the natural home

the natural home

STYLISH LIVING INSPIRED BY NATURE

Judith Wilson

jacqui small

First published in 2008 by Jacqui Small LLP,
an imprint of Aurum Press, 7 Greenland Street, London NW1 0ND

ISBN-13: 978 1 903221 97 6

A catalogue record for this book is available from the British Library.

2010 2009 2008
10 9 8 7 6 5 4 3 2 1

Printed in China

PUBLISHER Jacqui Small
COMMISSIONING EDITOR Jo Copestick
EDITORIAL MANAGER Judith Hannam
DESIGNER Ashley Western
EDITOR Hilary Mandleberg
PRODUCTION Peter Colley
PICTURE RESEARCH Nadine Bazar

contents

Think of the natural home, and what do you see? A tactile interior decked out in gleaming wood, perhaps, with textural linens and robust stone, smooth bamboo flooring or the opalescent gleam of mother-of-pearl. Yet how carefully do we also consider the natural world, from which all these wonderful items have been sourced, and how often do we remember its current state of decline? The fact is that, in today's more green-aware world, it's impossible to focus on decorating our homes without a serious look at adopting a more natural lifestyle.

Being eco-conscious has now become a political, moral and practical issue. If ever there was a time to change the way we treat our natural world, it's now. For the natural novice, it makes sense to start at home. Many of the world's CO_2 emissions come from the things we do every day, which is why energy is a hot topic. But the building materials we use are another hot topic – just a tiny percentage of these are recycled. The amount of energy it takes to make new building materials is enormous. That is why learning to adapt what we use, adopt recycled materials or choose elements from sustainable sources, becomes a crucial step in the journey to our natural home.

Yet for the design-conscious individual, there's still the worry that going natural means compromising on style and choice. Thankfully, it doesn't. High-street stores and specialist suppliers are falling over themselves to provide natural products, ranging from organic textiles to eco paints and from energy-efficient lightbulbs to low-flow showerheads, while contemporary designers are increasingly using recycled materials to dramatic effect. Going the natural route is no longer for the minority: today it makes ethical as well as beautiful and healthy good sense.

OPPOSITE One way of achieving a successful natural home is to combine the beauty of natural materials with cleverly salvaged furniture. In this room, exposed brickwork and wooden beams mix seamlessly with an antique leather chaise and vintage chairs. The natural effect helps to soften the loft space.

THIS PAGE When planning a natural home, a sensitive balance between retaining existing architectural features and adding new pieces is essential. This kitchen mixes an existing terracotta floor painted with a soft grey wash with shelves made from reclaimed scaffolding boards and a table converted from a tilt-top wine-tasting table.

Planning the Natural Home

As any experienced homeowner knows, perfect planning is the key to creating a beautiful but well-functioning home. Yet putting together a natural home requires particularly rigorous preparation. It isn't just about cosmetic changes but requires the development of a new mindset, which then needs to be translated into practical measures. Before you begin, you will need to do plenty of research.

It's vital, for instance, to find out what makes a house energy-efficient, what building materials should be avoided, how you can plan for the future and why recycling is an important issue.

When you have the information you need, it will be easier to crystallise your thoughts about what you want from your natural home. For most, it will be great style, but achieved using products from sustainable and/or recycled sources, and with a careful reining in of energy use. For many, a healthier home with an absence of harmful materials will also be a common goal. Others may want to go wholeheartedly down a 'green' route, hiring a green-minded architect or building a natural home from scratch.

Once you are committed to creating a natural home, you'll find that a new world opens up. Researching why you need to reduce carbon emissions or choosing materials for beauty and ethical good sense, will make the design process positively irresistible.

OPPOSITE ABOVE LEFT Plan to use local resources and materials so that the fabric of the building blends seamlessly with its location, as is the case in this South African house.

OPPOSITE ABOVE RIGHT Using antique or vintage furniture is the ultimate form of recycling. Look for pieces in beautiful timber, which will set a unique stamp on the interior as well as being 'green'.

OPPOSITE CENTRE LEFT Sourcing labour and materials locally reduces the carbon footprint of your home. Work on this African house was carried out by local craftsmen wherever possible.

OPPOSITE CENTRE RIGHT Plan new bathrooms to save water, from choosing a shower instead of a bath to fitting water-saving devices.

OPPOSITE BELOW LEFT Heating and lighting choices matter. A wood-burning stove is an eco alternative to an open fire.

OPPOSITE BELOW RIGHT Opt for architecture that will 'bring the outside in' as in this country house in Belgium with its giant windows.

THE NATURAL

PHILOSOPHY

For those of us who haven't previously been green-minded, or who have thought no more about natural materials than about their veritable good looks, making a commitment to the natural home can seem overwhelming. Establishing a personal philosophy is the first step. Open your eyes to the scale of the problem in our natural world. The media, the internet and campaign group websites are great places to bone up on the facts. Put simply, experts agree that carbon emissions – the result of burning fossil fuels like oil, coal and gas – are contributing to global warming, and that our natural resources are being ravaged by the world's demand for energy. It's not enough to let politicians and campaigners deal with the issues: we owe it to our children and grandchildren to take responsibility. Creating a natural home is a brilliant place to start.

This means that it's crucial to take the initiative and ask searching questions about the origins and composition of the new materials, furnishings and furniture that we pick for our homes, as well as to explore whether where we live is energy-efficient. Nowadays, the whole process is made easier by the example of some high-street retailers, who are publicly vowing to reduce their carbon footprint.

OPPOSITE Developing a green conscience is as much about what is retained in the home as what is added. In this modern open-plan space, the original brickwork is teamed with a modern sofa and vintage coffee table.

BELOW Choosing to go 'eco' can simply mean opting for natural materials as in this Norwegian lodge, with its tongue-and-groove panelling, linen blinds and timber floorboards.

PERSONAL QUESTIONS

Thinking through the issues can throw up some interesting personal questions. Learning to save energy is easy to understand, but accepting that ours has become a throwaway society, and resolving to buy less and recycle more, is a hard rule to follow. There will be other compromises, too. Choosing natural materials and eco-friendly energy sources sadly isn't the cheapest option. And are you prepared to forgo levels of luxury, such as not having a power shower or getting used to the less attractive illumination that is provided by low-energy light bulbs?

All these questions need to be answered before your new natural philosophy emerges. But whatever your final degree of commitment, don't beat yourself up if you only have the time and money for minor changes. Every little helps, and the greatest beneficiary will be you.

SHARE YOUR NEWLY FORMED NATURAL PHILOSOPHY WITH YOUR FRIENDS. THERE'S NOTHING LIKE COMPARING IDEAS WITH OTHER LIKE-MINDED INDIVIDUALS FOR ENERGISING AND EXPANDING ON A PERSONAL MANTRA

LOCATION

Where you live, be it in a rural setting or in the city, as well as the period, type and style of your property, will directly affect the way you plan your natural home. For example, for city dwellers, the introduction of natural materials can provide a welcome bridge between the urban landscape and an organic mood within, while a nineteenth-century cottage, in the depths of the countryside, may already boast beautiful brick and stone architecture, and can easily be decorated with natural, rustic textiles and recycled furniture. For those fortunate enough to be embarking on a new-build home, this may be the chance to site your house so you can maximise its views of the landscape, to use recycled local materials or even – provided there is sufficient space – to experiment with renewable energy such as a ground-source heat pump. Yet it may be less appropriate and sometimes impossible in a period or listed property, to introduce energy-saving measures such as solar panels.

ABOVE LEFT A hanging chair creates a quiet spot outdoors: however tiny the space, it is essential to create a link with the natural world.

LEFT In a city apartment, a roof terrace literally gives a window onto the outside world as well as creating good ventilation in summer.

OPPOSITE ABOVE LEFT Key colours from the external world can be cleverly woven into a room's colour scheme. This Australian house uses grass-green cushions to tie in with the garden outside.

OPPOSITE ABOVE RIGHT If building a new home, use existing vegetation as a focal point. This courtyard sitting zone has an enormous window that looks directly onto a well-established Aleppo pine tree.

OPPOSITE BELOW LEFT This modern double-height extension added to a city period house is screened by a mature tree and benefits from views of its foliage.

OPPOSITE BELOW RIGHT Placing key furniture pieces close to an outdoor area helps blend inside and out. This relaxed breakfast bar looks straight out onto the garden.

Creating a physical link between your home, and the natural world outside, is vital. For most of us, particularly city dwellers, the world has become a frantic place, filled with complex technology, man-made surfaces and unwelcome pollution. The simple sight of the natural world outside, be it a hillside or just sky and trees, is always to be cherished. If your property has great views, make the most of them. If it doesn't – and you are embarking on renovations – consider hiring an architect to help you plan your vistas.

There are also many simpler ways of forging a physical link between your available outside space, and indoors. French or sliding doors that open onto a garden or inner courtyard are ideal, while even a balcony or roof terrace will suffice in a city environment. Using materials that link indoors and out, such as slate flooring in both zones or bamboo wall panelling from garden to indoors, will help, too.

DECORATIVE INSPIRATION

Also consider taking inspiration from any natural elements that surround your property. For example, in a city flat with big windows and a direct view onto treetops, it's fun to keep the interior style modern and

LEFT Play with contrasts, using natural materials within to frame stunning views outside. In this English country bedroom, the rich grain of timber panelling is offset by the lush landscape beyond the floor-to-ceiling window.

OPPOSITE This modern tree house in South Africa was designed and built by its architect owner to deliberately blend with the surrounding forest. Giant picture windows frame the ever-changing foliage.

stark, but to put it together using sustainable wood and hessian as a subtle reference to the foliage outside. Alternatively, a period country cottage, already dominated by the muted, greys and browns of its stone and timber architecture, may be layered within using the brighter shades and textures of the exterior landscape, such as leaf greens, taupe and corn yellow.

Opting for a natural home also gives you the opportunity of getting into the habit of thinking local.

We may all be persuaded, in today's world of plenty, that we can have any surface or substance shipped from anywhere in the world. But is that ethically correct? It's in fact much better to source locally quarried stone, to use floorboards salvaged from a nearby demolition site or to have a fantastic dining table built to order by a local craftsman, using timber from a tree blown down in the garden. And by using local materials, your home will also feel more in keeping with its environment.

ENERGY

Worldwide, everyone is using far too much energy, but thankfully, with a little thought, we are all able to do something about it. By saving energy, and thus reducing our CO_2 emissions, we can help to slow global warming and preserve our world. So if it's a natural home you're after, rule number one is to reduce your energy consumption.

One reason for doing this is that, currently, only a tiny percentage of the electricity used in our homes is produced from a renewable energy source, while the rest is generated by burning fossil fuels and by nuclear power stations. By exploring the potential of your home to create some of its own energy, or by requesting a 'green' power tariff (an option you can choose whereby your energy supply company buys from a renewable energy source on your behalf), you can start to make a difference.

GET A HOME ENERGY CHECK

It's worth calling in an accredited energy assessor to do a 'home energy' check on your property. This will rate your home's impact on the environment in terms of its CO_2 emissions and will show you where there's room for improvement. In much of the developed world, local building regulations now insist that a building's carbon emissions fall below a certain level.

The first thing you can do, wherever possible, is update your electrical appliances. Look for models with a label stating their energy efficiency and – in the case of washing machines and dishwashers – their water consumption. Getting into the habit of making tiny changes, from switching off lights when they're not needed to only using the washing machine on a full load, and from not leaving appliances on standby to line-drying your washing, also makes a difference.

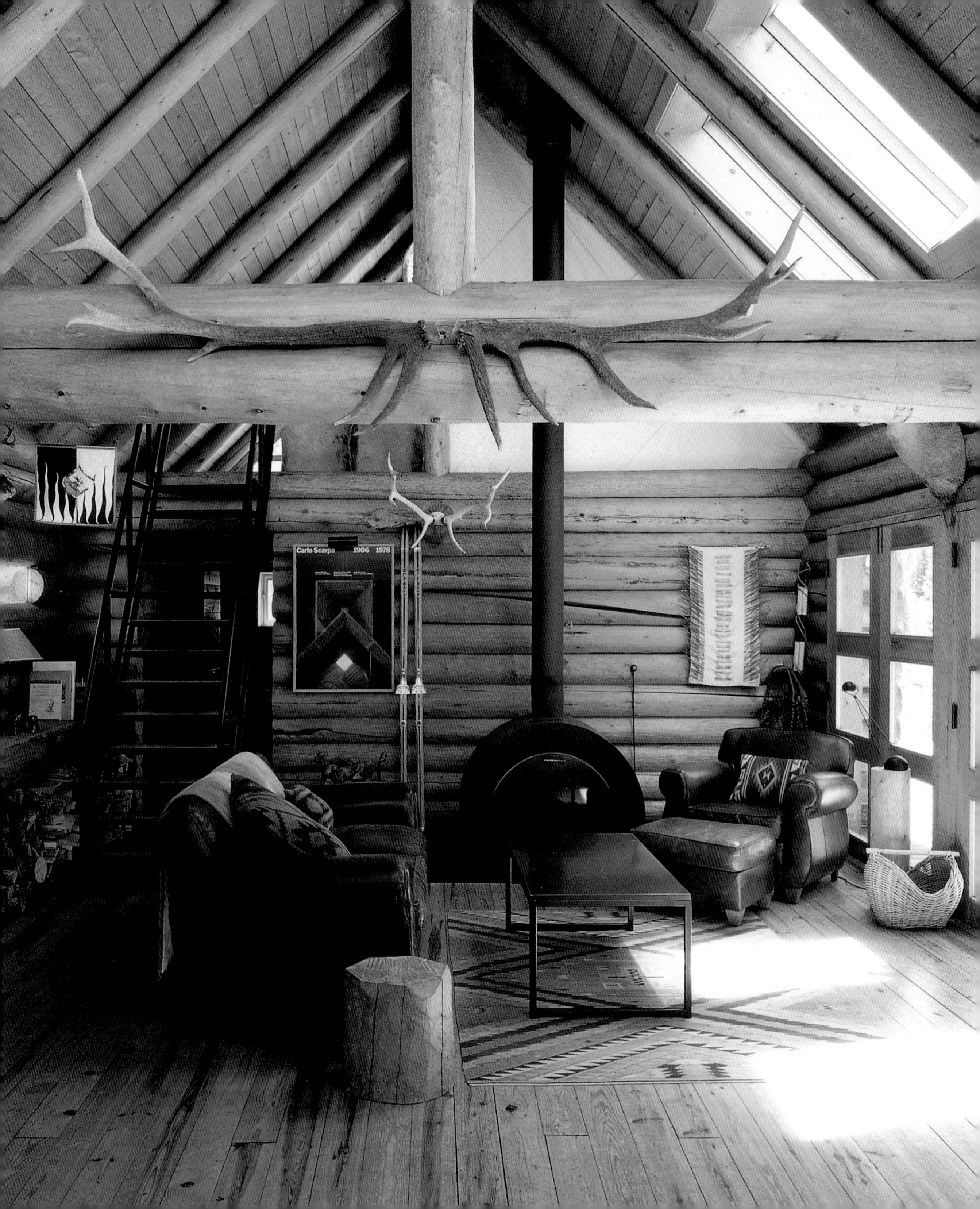
Carlo Scarpa 1906 1978

HEATING

While the ultimate in natural domestic heating comes from using renewable sources, such as wood-burning stoves and/or a ground-source heat pump (see page 28), many of us have to compromise and stick with a gas-fired central heating system. If that applies to you, you should ensure your system is up-to-date: an old boiler won't be energy-efficient and should be replaced with a high-efficiency condensing boiler.

You should also have an electronic timer, so the central heating and hot water can be set to come on at pre-arranged times, and you also need a programmable room thermostat. This ensures that when an optimum temperature is reached (20° C/68° F is ideal), the boiler prevents the central heating system from heating up further. In addition, thermostatic radiator valves give control over individual radiators, and your hot-water system should have its own separate thermostat (set no higher than 60° C/140° F).

Choosing a wood-burning stove, even if just for one room, can be a satisfying compromise in the natural home. Most use biomass fuel, produced from organic materials such as plant sources, and for domestic wood-burning stoves, this comes in the form of logs, wood pellets or chips. If possible, use a locally produced biomass fuel. Burning wood biomass fuel is regarded as being carbon neutral because it produces the same amount of carbon dioxide as it might if the wood were left to rot naturally in the forest. Moreover, wood-burning stoves also look beautiful and help create a cosy atmosphere at home.

INSULATION

However you choose to heat your home, it must be properly insulated, as half the heat loss in a typical house is through the walls and the loft. As well, therefore, as having cavity-wall insulation (or insulated board if your walls are solid), it's important to invest in loft insulation. Traditional insulation materials include mineral wool and fibreglass, but it's worth investigating natural insulating materials, from fire-retardant recycled newspaper to Thermafleece, which is made from British sheep's wool. Double-glazed windows are also a worthwhile investment, as they can cut by half the heat loss from windows. Double glazing works by trapping air between two panes of glass and creating an insulating barrier. The cost is generally around £3000 ($6000 at time of writing) for an average house.

MOVE ON FROM THE DESIGN-STATEMENT BATHROOM. THE PRIORITY IS CHOOSING WATER-SAVING FITTINGS, THEN SELECTING A RANGE OF GOOD-LOOKING NATURAL SURFACES

SAVING WATER

On average, each and every one of us uses 150 litres (40 U.S. gal.) of water per day, two-thirds of which is in the bathroom. With the changes in our weather patterns, it is imperative for us all to be more water-aware. so in the natural home, you should focus on water-saving measures in the bathroom.

For example, it's more eco-friendly to shower than take a bath, but that doesn't mean banning the bath entirely. Alternate bathing with showering, and don't overfill the bath, because a full bath can use over 80 litres (21 U.S. gal.), while a 5-minute shower only uses around 60 litres (14 U.S. gal.). Even better, buy a shower timer. A three-minute drenching uses just 35 litres (9 U.S. gal.).

Some shower manufacturers are now introducing eco showers, which restrict water flow. Then there is an aerated version, which reduces water flow but maintains pressure. It's also possible to fit a flow restrictor to a basin tap.

The toilet is one of the biggest water wasters. If you have an older model – which may use up to 10 litres (3 U.S. gal.) of water per flush – it's well worth replacing the cistern with one that incorporates a modern dual-flush system. This features a split button, which offers a choice of a full flush or a mini-flush. It's also possible to buy a device from specialist bathroom stores that can be retro-fitted to your cistern to provide a dual flush.

Another option is to consider fitting a water-saving device in the cistern. This is a brick-like object that sits in the cistern and, in a cistern with a 9–12 litre (2–3 U.S. gal.) capacity, can reduce the amount of water needed to flush by 1–3 litres (0.25–0.8 U.S. gal.).

LIGHTING

Over the last decade there has been a sea change in our attitude to lighting. Where once a central pendant light supplemented by table lamps sufficed, we now indulge in multiple overhead low-voltage halogen lights, plus task lighting and mood lighting. The result may look wonderful, but all these lights use a great deal of energy and even many 'so-called' low-voltage halogen lights actually need a transformer to work. In the natural home, we all need to adopt a greener approach to lighting. At its most basic, that means reducing the number of lights we install, and learning to switch off the lights when we leave a room.

It's also possible to switch to low-energy light bulbs. There has been much debate about the need to phase out traditional incandescent tungsten filament light bulbs, which waste energy by turning it into heat rather than light. Countries such as Australia have already banned them but in most parts of the world, the type of light bulb you buy is down to personal choice.

Energy-saving bulbs, otherwise called CFLs (compact fluorescent lamps), last 12 times longer than a conventional light bulb and, because they use around one-fifth of the energy of an ordinary 60-watt bulb, only require 13 to 18 watts. CFLs work in the same way as fluorescent lights. An electric current passes through gas in a tube, making the gas glow brightly while the bulb remains cool to the touch. However, low-energy bulbs don't always fit into conventional light fittings, though some designer lighting shops now offer fittings that are suitable for both types of bulbs. Other disadvantages are that CFLs are expensive to buy, most of them can't be used with dimmer switches and they produce a colder, less attractive light.

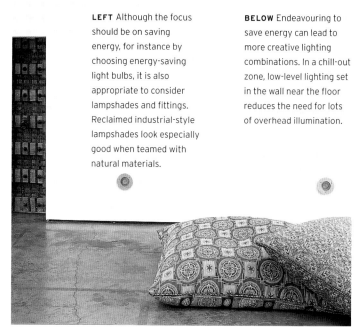

LEFT Although the focus should be on saving energy, for instance by choosing energy-saving light bulbs, it is also appropriate to consider lampshades and fittings. Reclaimed industrial-style lampshades look especially good when teamed with natural materials.

BELOW Endeavouring to save energy can lead to more creative lighting combinations. In a chill-out zone, low-level lighting set in the wall near the floor reduces the need for lots of overhead illumination.

THIS PAGE Maximising natural daylight is an important way of reducing the use of electric light at home. On this mezzanine floor, clever cut-out and folding timber panels let in daylight yet maintain a sense of privacy.

INTO THE FUTURE

Ground-Source Heat Pumps
These work by using a length of buried pipe filled with a mixture of water and anti-freeze. As the mixture is pumped through the pipe, heat is absorbed from the ground and is transferred into the home's hot water tank from where it provides space heating and hot water. Ground-source heat pumps are most suitable for use with underfloor heating or for low-temperature radiators, as they only raise the temperature to a maximum of 40° C (104° F), while conventional radiators require 60° C (140° F). The beauty of the system is that it needs only a minimum amount of electricity. Its disadvantages are that it's expensive, that you need a large site for the underground trench, and that installing it is a specialist operation.

Solar Energy
The power produced by solar panels can either be linked to the national grid or can be used as an independent off-grid system. They use a photovoltaic (PV) system: cells in the panels convert sunlight into electricity. When light shines onto a cell it creates an electric field across its layers and causes electricity to flow. Solar panels are particularly satisfying because they use free energy from the sun. However, they are still comparatively expensive to fit, may need planning permission and must be placed on a roof or a wall that faces 90 per cent south.

Wind Turbines
The most basic domestic wind turbine has aerodynamic blades that use wind to create electricity. The beauty of it is that wind is a free, renewable source of energy, and does not give out any CO_2 emissions. Like solar power, the energy that a wind turbine produces can be connected to the national grid, but wind turbines are also good for homes in off-grid locations. For most of us, however, using a wind turbine is not yet a feasible option: to work properly, it needs to be located on the top of a hill where there are strong, consistent wind speeds, and it is also expensive to install.

Green or 'Living' Roofs
The grass (actually a mix of lichens and moss) in a green, or 'living' roof provides a habitat for wildlife in cities and helps combat global warming by reducing the amount of CO_2 in the air. Green roofs help insulate buildings and also alleviate flooding because they absorb excess rainfall. A living roof must be installed by a specialist contractor.

THIS PAGE Whether a home is new-build or a period property, it's important to investigate the potential for using energy from renewable sources. A ground-source heat pump is a good choice for underfloor heating in a home with a stone floor.

OPPOSITE The popularity of green or 'living' roofs is growing, not just among ecologists, but also among architects and designers. As well as the fact that they give buildings better thermal performance, living roofs can improve the air quality in cities and create greener spaces generally.

OPPOSITE There is a vast range of natural paints available these days, so it makes sense to paint walls with low-VOC paints. Most come in a range of gentle, natural-looking hues.

RIGHT Where possible, make eco choices when selecting materials. This converted barn in Norfolk uses plenty of timber for a natural, rustic and healthy environment.

AVOIDING

TOXINS

The focus of a natural home is beautiful, natural materials, but it's also crucial to remove, or to avoid adding, harmful substances. We all want to live in a healthy environment, so taking time to research the materials you plan to use is worth the effort. Choosing 'eco' versions of some common building materials will be more expensive, but what price good health?

VOLATILE ORGANIC COMPOUNDS

Paints have come in for much criticism recently and the rise of 'natural' paints continues apace. The main culprits in mainstream paints are the Volatile Organic Compounds (VOCs) that are contained in the solvents used. When a room is painted, these solvents evaporate, giving off an unpleasant 'new paint' smell: it is these gases that are potentially toxic. For a more natural environment, it therefore makes sense to use organic, natural or eco paints. Natural paints still contain VOCs but at much reduced levels, so read the label on the tin.

Unlike mainstream paints, they are more likely to use natural raw ingredients, such as plant and mineral pigments, and they are usually also biodegradable.

FORMALDEHYDE

Once the darling of the DIY scene and used for everything from kitchen cupboards to furniture, MDF (medium-density fibreboard) has also come in for criticism in recent years. It is a type of strong hardboard that is less expensive than wood. However, due to the amount of formaldehyde resin that is used to bond the board together, it, together with chipboard, plywood and hardboard, will continuously 'off-gas' into the home. The most natural alternative is to choose recycled timber in place of MDF and its relatives, but it is also possible to source formaldehyde-free MDF as well as hardboard that is made from recycled wood waste. These will be more expensive, but your home will be a healthier place as a result.

RECYCLING

We may all have been guilty of wanting the newest, shiniest objects for our home, but who hasn't also been appalled at the thought of perfectly good kitchens and interior fittings being removed from houses, just because they are out of date? It is finally seeping into mainstream thinking that recycling offers a greener, more creative solution. The manufacture of new building materials and the cost of transporting them all contributes to CO_2 emissions and takes its toll on the natural world. Isn't it better to look afresh at what we already have, to repair or adapt, and to enjoy the history that recycled things bring to the home? By not throwing things away in the first place, or by choosing recycled surfaces and fittings, we also keep our already stretched landfill sites clearer.

At its most basic, recycling building materials means taking items that might otherwise have been regarded as waste and reusing them. These can range from items such as yellow stock bricks and reclaimed timbers, to a

ABOVE LEFT Using antique or junk-shop furniture in mellow, natural materials is not only the ultimate form of recycling, but creates a one-off look.

ABOVE To highlight unusual recycled pieces, keep to a neutral colour scheme. In this off-white room, all attention is focused on the old plank table supported on an industrial base.

OPPOSITE LEFT There is satisfaction in creating a new kitchen design out of recycled surfaces and fittings: here the mix of stone worktops and ceramic sink gives a pure and simple finish.

OPPOSITE RIGHT Not all recycled fittings, such as bathtubs, need to be restored to a pristine state. Worn, gently distressed pieces have a distinct charm, especially when they are teamed with raw natural materials.

beautiful old parquet floor, perhaps salvaged from a school, or a stone mantelpiece from a demolition site. If you are restoring, or adding to, a period home, it makes sense to use recycled building materials appropriate to the architecture. But even a new-build house can be built from reused components.

The best hunting grounds for anything from a recycled bath to an entire salvaged floor or from old radiators to second-hand bricks, are nearby demolition sites and salvage yards. By going local you will also save on the cost of transportation. However, if you are likely to need a large quantity of materials or some very specific item, take time to find a reclamation dealer who will be able to source it for you.

Two downsides, however, of using recycled materials are that advance planning is crucial and you need to be adaptable. It may take time to find what you are looking for: for instance, what you want may not be available in exactly the right quantities or you may not

get a perfect match. Another downside is that not all recycled materials are cheaper than their new equivalents. Some very beautiful salvage fittings and surfaces can be prohibitively expensive.

'REPURPOSED' ITEMS

Many recycled pieces may be 'repurposed'. For instance, several chunky railway sleepers might be used to create wonderful shelves, or a marble slab, salvaged from a fishmonger's shop, could be cut down and used as a bathroom vanity worktop. Once you adopt a creative mindset, the possibilities are endless.

To help you adapt recycled materials and create new fittings, it's important to find a creative joiner or builder. Seek out furniture makers who might be prepared to create new furniture using recycled elements, from a headboard made from old flooring planks to a dining table made from an old enamelled sign. Or look at some of the eco websites where you can buy innovative furniture, from coffee tables made from recycled washing-machine drums to sustainable cardboard shelving.

It is also worth researching new surfaces that are made from recycled elements. These days there are some wonderfully inventive examples around. They include bricks and tiles made from recycled glass, sheets of rubber made from recycled Wellington boots and suitable for use as table coverings, bar-stool coverings or waterproof mats for kitchens and bathrooms, and even a highly durable sheet material made from soybeans and recycled newspapers that can be used for covering units, tables and walls. Creating slick modern designs using recycled surfaces gives designers immense freedom and you will be safe in the knowledge that they contain natural elements, too.

OPPOSITE Recycled architectural features, particularly old timber beams, can be used to stunning effect for shelves, stair treads or to create new furniture. Here, bleached, aged timber beams provide solid storage for crockery.

THIS PAGE In this barn in France, updated to provide a contemporary living space, there is a preponderance of natural materials: walls are a mix of terracotta tiles and stone with wonderful sturdy old beams.

THIS PAGE Use a mix-and-match approach to bind together disparate pieces of recycled furniture and salvaged surfaces. Here, aged terracotta tiles and an old timber table both have a weathered patina that is set off by the blue-painted vintage chairs.

The recycled kitchen

- Robust recycled materials can be cut to fit and 'repurposed' as worktops.

- Scour salvage yards for original timber 1930s and 1950s kitchen cabinets to create a vintage look.

- Rethink the island unit: a school refectory table or old pine kitchen table are perfect.

- Reclaimed flooring, from parquet tiles to antique boards, is durable and ages well.

Creating a new kitchen using recycled materials salves the eco conscience and produces a unique look. Who wants a fitted modern kitchen like everyone else's? 'Repurposing' makes practical sense. Materials and furniture that have survived decades will continue to serve you well. Research all potential elements before planning. Lengths of salvaged iroko, pitch pine or marble can be cut to size, but specific key pieces, such as an oak library bookcase that you want to reuse as a dresser, will need to have its dimensions checked so the rest of the kitchen fits around it. Excellent hunting grounds for kitchen elements are salvage centres, reclamation yards or specialist companies who make bespoke furniture using reclaimed materials.

ABOVE AND RIGHT In place of new fitted cupboards, experiment with salvaged timber bookcases or recycled planks used as shelving, and integrate them into a utility-style kitchen.

THIS PAGE In a new-build South African beach house, simple but contrasting natural textures and scaled-up local ethnic accessories are combined with clean lines to create a very modern look.

Natural Style

Trends these days are gratifyingly varied and no one should feel constrained by a particular fashion. It is as acceptable to opt for a sleek, modern interior as for a gently distressed country design, incorporating more directional looks, from twentieth-century vintage to decorative eclectic, along the way. Choosing to create a natural home shouldn't compromise your style choices: if anything, it should enhance them. The difference is that you can underpin the key styles by thoughtful sourcing of the appropriate materials and furniture. Gone are the days when going 'natural' meant adding indiscriminate yellow pine panelling and tie-dyed cheesecloth to your decorative scheme. Today's chic looks have natural materials as their cornerstone.

It's important to define your preferred style at the very outset. The architecture of your home may dictate a particular look. A modern flat may cry out for honed marble and sleek sustainable oak, while flinty local slate and crunchy organic cottons might be the best choice for a seaside cottage. Next, look carefully at the detail of your home: what beautiful natural surfaces can be added to play up attractive, original features? Is there anything man-made that jars and should be removed? What is your own characteristic interior style, or is now the moment to try a fresh look? Once the style you are after has crystallised, then it's easy to pick and choose appropriate natural elements to pull it all together.

OPPOSITE TOP LEFT Rounded shapes inspired by the contours of the natural world create softness in a pared-down bathroom.

OPPOSITE TOP RIGHT Painted tongue-and-groove panelling, relaxed furniture choices and a fresh blue-and-white colour scheme create a Natural Coastal mood.

OPPOSITE CENTRE LEFT Mix and match unusual, gently distressed old pieces for a rustic finish and a Natural Country style.

OPPOSITE CENTRE RIGHT Simplicity of line and a neutral colour scheme play up period architecture. In this attic bedroom, rustic furniture also sets the tone.

OPPOSITE BELOW LEFT The mix of natural materials and sharp, modern contours have a satisfying allure. Here, a sleek oak headboard contrasts with high-tech metal bedside lighting.

OPPOSITE BELOW RIGHT A glittering chandelier and giant photos contrasting with chunky logs and a stone fireplace perfectly deliver Natural Decorative style.

THIS PAGE This modern
seaside holiday home is
decorated with cutting-
edge simplicity. While iroko
cantilevered stairs set a
modern tone, the relaxing
banquette seating is
upholstered with textural
natural calico.

NATURAL MODERN

The notion of using natural materials to create modern good
looks may seem a contradictory one. After all, the Modernists of the
twentieth century believed in making the most of contemporary possibilities,
and that often meant choosing innovative man-made materials suitable for
mass-production. By contrast, there is the legacy of the 1950s, when the
Scandinavian Modern look – which depended upon sculptural forms and
natural materials – took hold. Many of today's architects have tapped into
that aesthetic, combining a celebration of natural materials with sleek lines.
In fact, modern and natural can happily combine, and it's perfectly possible at
home to marry a desire for the latest technologies, a powerful sense of
geometry, and the use of pure materials.

When opting for cutting-edge style, it's important to define your own
interpretation of modern. For most people, that will mean regularity and
order, with straight lines, squared-off furniture silhouettes and expanses of
sleek, smooth surfaces, from worktops to wall panelling. Some of you may
still be attracted by the pared-down rigours of minimalist style, while others
will prefer a softer approach, adding in some gentle organic shapes as
contrast. Most of all, it is the choice of surfaces, the careful selection of
contours and detailing and the way they are combined together that will
create the perfect fusion of modern and natural.

ARCHITECTURAL FEATURES

A modern interior depends on clean-cut, beautifully defined spaces to give it a contemporary look, even if the property itself is a period building. There should generally be an absence of fussy detailing such as mouldings, cupboard doors should be flush with minimal ornament, and dominant features, such as the staircase, should be strong and simple in style. One or two imposing architectural features, such as a double-height ceiling or a mezzanine level, will set a particularly cutting-edge stamp.

Well-defined architectural detailing is just as possible to achieve using natural materials. Glass, steel and concrete are not friends of the natural home, so endeavour to limit, or even banish, them. Instead, you could create a wonderful cantilevered staircase using recycled railway sleepers or any new local wood from an accredited sustainable source. In place of a wall of flush MDF cupboards, consider timber doors made from wood with an exceptional grain, though this will be a considerable investment, and you may need to save money elsewhere.

SHAPE

The shape and contours of furniture, fittings and even window treatments play a major role. To enhance the

modern feel, pick upholstered pieces that feature clean-cut rectangular lines, furniture, and especially kitchen units, with cubic shapes, and curtains or blinds in a clean-cut linear mood. Roller or Roman blinds, or shutters, look more appropriate than gathered curtains. Aim for a lean silhouette when it comes to surfaces, too. Opt for the regular horizontal lines of timber floorboards, or giant slabs on floors, and uninterrupted stretches of stone or wood worktop, rather than a small-scale grid of tiles on splashbacks or floors.

Today's version of modern also gives a definite nod to fluid lines and organic shapes. This is entirely appropriate in the natural home: think of the satisfying oval of an egg, or the bumpy, rounded contours of sea-washed pebbles or seed pods. One or two carefully selected pieces of furniture, with similarly gentle contours – such as a curve-backed beech dining chair or rounded woven leather pouffes – will add a relaxed mood. Curves are perfectly achievable without resorting to man-made substances such as plastic. Think of the contour of a walnut bentwood barstool or a one-off organically shaped ceramic lamp base with a recycled paper drum shade. The same is also true when it comes to bathroom fittings. The rounded oval of a travertine basin, or a limestone bath in an egg shape, will create a very satisfying addition to a modern setting.

OPPOSITE LEFT This new-build family home in the Channel Islands blends dramatic ceiling volume and industrial-style lighting with the mellow colour and texture of a timber-clad ceiling.

OPPOSITE RIGHT In this Australian house, built along minimalist lines and furnished with careful simplicity, the presence of the great outdoors and the choice of curved dining chairs, perfectly blends natural with modern.

RIGHT Starkly simple contemporary architecture can be unforgiving but is easily tempered by the inclusion of just one stunning natural surface. Here, the rich colour and grain of the wooden floor warm up the pure white of the walls.

THIS PAGE A contemporary architectural shell looks very effective teamed with natural surfaces. In this South African beachside home, limed wooden cabinetry and a bleached-out colour scheme look cosy yet modern.

OPPOSITE LEFT The blend of modern sanitary ware and sleek, timber surfaces looks dramatic. In this Colorado home, southern yellow pine on walls, ceiling and floor highlights the smooth contours of a contemporary bath.

OPPOSITE RIGHT Introducing occasional highly textured accessories can add bite to a cool, pared-down interior. Here, a contemporary double globe Thai basket-weave shade softens the clean lines of a modern kitchen.

TEXTURE

Precisely because modern style requires clean-cut edges and simplicity, it's vital to get the textures right. Too many plain surfaces and the interior will look clinical and boring; too many rough textures and the sense of modernity will escape. There should be a balance between showing off the excitingly unruly, varied textures and inherent patterns found in natural substances – such as the light pitting of a chocolate-coloured travertine or tiny fossils in a piece of limestone – and adding a certain sleek, sophisticated finish.

Choose stone surfaces such as marble or granite, either with a highly polished gloss or honed for a subtler sheen, rather than the textured finish of riven slate which is more approriate for a true rustic look. Wooden worktops, floorboards or panelling with a comparatively simple grain should also be chosen, then finished with natural oil, rather than being brushed

(which usually involves wire-brushing the wood to highlight the natural structure of the grain), as this finish may look too rustic. Look at a range of woods: beech or ash, for example, has a more sophisticated appearance than pine. For those wanting the elegance of a dark wood, use a dark stain on a locally sourced wood, rather than import an exotic hardwood and risk plundering a rainforest. For a seamless look on the walls, which might normally be achieved with the Modern aesthetic by using a cement-based product, opt for natural eco paints in cool, pale colours or go for a natural polished plaster finish.

Finally, do add in a dash of bumpy, irregular contrast for interest. The occasional bench fashioned from a chunk of hewn driftwood or a modern boxy sofa covered with the rough, irregular weave of fabric made from banana fibre and teamed with aluminium legs, may be all that is necessary to add contrast and excitement.

COLOUR

An emphasis on white and muted, sober neutrals is key
to achieving the Natural Modern look. As well as white
and off-whites, you could consider palest gull greys
through to silvery tones, or darker variations on this
theme, such as anthracite or blue-black. These cool
grey-toned colours look very sophisticated when they
are teamed with the warmer hues of wood. But you
should not forget bright accent shades either, as these
give the scheme a lift. Either a single chair upholstered
in tangerine wool or a lime green tiled wall would
produce the desired effect.

DETAILING

It is the smaller details just as much as the larger
statements that define modern style. Start with the
architectural fittings such as door and cupboard
handles, light switches and electric sockets. If you want
to up the modern ante and create a deliberate contrast
to the rich grain or texture of stone and wood
elsewhere, then use stainless steel, satin chrome or
polished nickel plate fittings in simple, linear shapes.
Alternatively, contrast pared-down, monastic natural
surfaces with textural fittings, from leather-covered
curtain poles and finials to a ceramic blind pull on a
leather cord or a solid oak body for a light switch.

Apply the same principles to light fittings and
lamps. Very modern steel and nickel table or wall lamps
create a wonderful contrast when set against a highly
patterned wood-grain or leather-upholstered wall. But
for a more natural contrast to simple surfaces, look for
table and floor lamps that are made from unusual
materials: think of a woven palm lamp base, a chic
rectangular mock croc leather lamp base or a floor
lamp with a stem made of bamboo.

THIS PAGE In a simple, minimalist sitting room featuring stark straight lines, modern classic furniture and contemporary lighting, the presence of a giant piece of driftwood creates a dramatic contrast. The detail provided by the snakeskin and wool cushions adds extra texture and registers more subtly.

THIS PAGE In this sitting room, a mid-toned stone-coloured paint exactly matches the simple, textural curtains yet gently contrasts with the blonder wood of the furniture and accessories. Accented with accessories in dark, sombre materials, the effect is elegant and pulled-together.

Natural paints and colours

- Natural colours don't have to be pale. Add just one deep shade, such as flinty grey or warm heather. It will look dramatic on cupboard doors, skirting or architraves.

- Neutrals can be cool or warm. Grey- and blue-toned neutrals work well in a sunny, south-facing room; buttery creams and toffee shades will warm up a room that is north-facing.

- Colour isn't just for walls: try experimenting with pale grey, string or olive shades on ceilings or floors.

Read the labels carefully when choosing natural paints. Eco-friendly paints use natural raw materials and plant or mineral pigments, and should contain a minimum of VOCs. Choose a range with a wide variety of colours and always ask for a hand-painted sample or a tester pot so you can check at home how the colour works in natural light. Also ensure that your chosen colours tone well with any natural surfaces in the room, such as wood or stone. You can experiment by choosing a mid-toned, a dark, and a pale version of a particular colour, then using it on the walls, floor and woodwork respectively. Alternatively, pick two or three similarly toned natural colours – try mushroom pink teamed with grey-blue – and use them on different walls for a gentle contrast.

ABOVE Stick to gentle paint tones that have an alliance to the natural colours we see in the landscape. Soft grey-blue, lilac and palest olive green, mixed with neutrals, are all wonderful choices.

RIGHT In an older property, gently textured plaster can be a good choice to disguise bumpy walls. Work in some textured timber furniture and distressed leather to complete the look.

NATURAL COUNTRY

The essence of pure country style combines a sense of relaxation and comfort with a respect for indigenous, rustic materials – some of which may be decades, even centuries, old. The boundaries of country style have become blurred in recent years. Natural Country hovers between 'modern country', which offers an extreme, pared-down take on rustic, and 'shabby chic', which combines a gently distressed look with a variety of homespun textures. In Natural Country style, key elements include tactile fabrics, robust materials such as timber and brick and, above all, a keenness to reflect the home inside with the great outdoors by mimicking nature's inherent soft colours and variegated patterns.

ABOVE Take decorative cues from existing period architecture. In this Belgian kitchen, rough plastered walls and terracotta tiles have prompted the choice of a chunky wood kitchen table and a rustic stone sink.

RIGHT Sensitive restoration is often the key to retaining wonderful old features, and in this way there is often no need to buy new building materials. In this old farmhouse and adjoining stable, beautiful herringbone brickwork and tiled floors are teamed with plain tongue-and-groove walls.

ABOVE There are multiple benefits to choosing local stone for an interior. As well as being more eco-friendly, the hues of the stonework in this relaxed sitting room have been used to inspire a muted, natural colour scheme.

ARCHITECTURE

Most country period properties have at least some of their 'bare bones' on show, and this, after all, is half the charm of a country home. A worn flagstone floor, gently sloping after countless footsteps, antique wooden rafters or an original lime-plastered wall are all features to be treasured and highlighted, so if your home possesses any of these, take them as your starting point for a Natural Country style. Where such elements are missing, consider adding sympathetically to the architecture that already exists. Carefully blended, a reclaimed oak floor or a salvaged front door will add extra character yet look as if it has always been there, or recycled building materials, used for a new extension to an old property, can help blur the boundaries between period and modern.

OPPOSITE For a relaxed country style, a mix-and-match approach is ideal. Wonderful antiques, such as these old Transvaal chairs, can be unified using honest, simple fabrics like gingham or ticking.

RIGHT If country period architecture is particularly dominant, as in this room with its complex chestnut-beam roof structure, it is important to choose furniture with a strong character. Cabriole leg detailing and an ornate antique bed hold their own well here.

FURNITURE

Choosing furniture in an appropriate country style, particularly antique pieces, is one of the fastest short cuts to creating a Natural Country style. This is not the place for over-polished antiques but for a collection of good, solid pieces created from natural components like timber, stone and leather that have withstood the test of time. Look for gentle contours, from the curve of a cabriole leg to an over-stuffed Chesterfield: for a plainer look, chunky styles like a giant oak dresser or a scrubbed pine table can form the basis of a good collection. Selecting furniture is not about faithfully matching historical periods or shapes: rather, aim for a varied mix and match, giving the impression the interior has evolved organically over time.

It's particularly satisfying to pick a wonderful, worn piece of timber furniture. Look for an enticing grain and also for patina that has been created from decades of use and polish. Antique hand-crafted pieces, from a wobbly old milking stool to a grain chest, are all the better for minor irregularities. If you have the pick of plenty of hand-me-down family antiques, then enjoy. For those starting from scratch, scour antique fairs and junk stores to put together an enterprising mix. Remember that giving a new home to cast-off furniture is the ultimate form of recycling.

A simpler, clean-lined version of Natural Country can also be achieved by choosing new furniture but before you buy, ask plenty of searching questions about the manufacture of each piece and the provenance of the wood. For example, new upholstered furniture should be crafted according to traditional methods, with solid wood frames, coil springs and wool wadding plus feather-and-down cushion fillings. Then again, you might like to commission one of the many designers around who create modern rustic pieces using beautiful woods or a specialist joiner who will be happy to use wood that comes from reclaimed sources.

FABRICS

Choose dense, cocooning natural fabrics to play up the natural mood and create tactile emphasis. In a country home where good-looking style needs to co-exist with children, animals and the great outdoors, practical textiles matter. Smart upholstery choices include linen union, denim, wool and enduring horsehair, though basics like hessian also blend in well and cotton canvas is great for lightweight loose covers on dining chairs. Also, aim to combine crunchy textures with finer ones and try and bring in a gentle mix of stripes, checks and faded florals.

For Natural Country window dressings, choose lined full-length curtains and hang them from a chunky wooden pole. Heavy linens, hemp, cotton and linen unions are excellent choices. Roman or roll-up blinds give a simpler look than curtains, or choose plain fabric panels, strung from a pole with leather thongs or jute string. Finer cottons, rough linens, muslin or ginghams are all appropriate choices for such panels. Recycled fabric is another wonderful addition to the natural home. Antique linen sheets can be dyed and stitched into curtains or used as tablecloths, while vintage mattress ticking can be teamed with patchwork floral fabrics to make unusual cushions.

BELOW LEFT Choose highly textural, rustic-looking fabrics either to blend with furniture or for a deliberate contrast. Here, chic raffia cushions are a foil to the chunky weave of the armchairs.

OPPOSITE ABOVE LEFT Careful choice of fabric can add a softer, more relaxed touch in a country kitchen. Here, natural fabric panels replace door fronts and lend a simple elegance.

OPPOSITE ABOVE RIGHT Linens and cottons in their unbleached, off-white state look particularly appropriate in a country setting. Look out for antique linen sheets that can be hung as curtains.

OPPOSITE BELOW LEFT Using antique tablelinens can be the ultimate in recycling. Pure linen, often decorated with cutwork, embroidery or monogramming, softens beautifully with age and lasts a long time.

OPPOSITE BELOW RIGHT The Natural Country look is pared down and easy to live with. Keep to a simple heading style for linen, cotton or wool curtains and hang from a plain metal or wooden pole.

THIS PAGE Bare plastered walls add a comforting, warm atmosphere to a country property, especially in a large room. It is possible to add pigment to plaster: in this house in Belgium, wheat-coloured plastered walls are complemented by natural flooring.

COLOUR

Keep colours muted, rather than jarringly bright, taking your inspiration from the natural landscape. In an interior with plenty of wood and stone, it feels calmer to complement those surfaces with gentle tones, from pale cream to deep butterscotch, contrasted with dark accents such as chocolate or a dark grey. For a more colourful look, add small quantities of richer shades, from moss green to berry reds.

SURFACES

When choosing wall surfaces, work with the elements you have. For example, if your walls are slightly uneven, use muted organic paints to accentuate the natural highlights and shadows. Where replastering is necessary, consider using a natural, eco-friendly lime plaster that allows walls to breathe and is long-lasting. Wood-panelled walls also suit a country setting. Avoid Seventies-style yellow pine, though, and instead choose recycled wood panelling from an architectural salvage yard. Alternatively, buy inexpensive new pine, which can be painted with natural paints or stains.

Floors and worktops require the appropriate textures and patterns. In a truly rustic home, opt for highly textural surfaces such as riven slate that features split, uneven surfaces and is available in colours ranging from pale grey to black or dark green. For a warmer finish on the floor, choose naturally uneven reclaimed boards. A more sophisticated version of Natural Country can be achieved with smooth, regular new wooden floorboards, but choose wood that has dramatic graining or obvious knotting. Ask for a brushed finish (see page 47) and protect with a natural wood oil rather than with varnish. Stone floor choices include limestone, terracotta tiles, or even cork, with its natural colour gradations and light pitting.

NATURAL RETRO

The term 'retro' was first coined in the Seventies, to describe nostalgia for recently past styles and tastes, but the trend for using twentieth-century retro – whether from the Thirties, Fifties or Seventies – has, in the last decade, taken the interiors world by storm. For some, dipping into retro merely constitutes adding a few pieces to what they already have: a vintage Danish rosewood sideboard, perhaps, or some 1930s cracked leather armchairs, mixed in with contemporary natural furniture and fittings. For others, tapping into the materials and colours beloved by our parents and grandparents is part of the grand scheme.

Opting for a natural retro theme is comparatively easy and using vintage pieces is, of course, the ultimate form of recycling. However, just because

ABOVE LEFT This dining room has all the elements of a perfect retro room: Modernist-inspired clean lines, taupe-painted wood panelling and 1950s chairs, together with glass doors overlooking the great outdoors.

LEFT If you happen to have a treasured collection of vintage twentieth-century furniture – such as these Cherner chairs in a New York apartment – design the room as a contrast. Here, expanses of dark wood panelling are perfect.

OPPOSITE This living room in Denmark combines all the elements favoured by the Scandinavian Modern movement: clean lines, a neutral colour scheme, and a mix of natural materials, including leather, wood, cane and sisal.

furniture is second hand doesn't mean that it is natural.
The plastics and man-made substances much beloved
by the designers of the Sixties and Seventies, for
example, are best avoided. The influences to look to are
primarily the mood (though not necessarily the
materials) of the Modernist movement, from the
Thirties to the Fifties, and the Scandinavian Modern
movement that had its heyday in the Fifties.

ARCHITECTURE AND LAYOUT

For some, an authentic Modernist house is the ultimate
retro choice, with its giant picture windows taking in
the landscape, its open-plan spaces, its streamlined
layout and its emphasis on light. We can't all live that
dream but there are ways to tweak existing architecture
to create a similar framework. A new kitchen/living-
room extension, for example, can be designed with
floor-to-ceiling windows looking onto the garden, or
internal walls can be removed to create a flowing open-
plan space. Ornamentation, such as mouldings, should
be minimal, and rather than removing decorative
features, painting them to match the walls minimises
their impact and helps create a streamlined look.

SURFACES

Walls should be treated with simplicity. The Modernists
favoured plain painted walls in white or palest neutrals,
so pick out natural paints in subtle tones to create a
similar mood. The Scandinavian Moderns also aimed
for a streamlined look, but preferred to use natural
materials on their walls. An entire wall of timber
tongue-and-groove panelling, either painted or left
plain to show off an attractive grain, would look
appropriately authentic, but try to avoid tongue-and-
groove panelled ceilings, which can be overpowering
and is redolent of Seventies yellow pine ceilings.

THIS PAGE This 1950s
Florida home boasts the
type of architecture that
made Modernism so
popular. Giant floor-to-
ceiling windows bring the
outdoors inside, while
natural textural details,
from the wool carpet to
the timber detailing, give
the neutral colour scheme
something of a lift.

To emphasise simplicity and to play up the flowing, open-plan nature of the space, you should keep the flooring plain. Timber floorboards in pale woods such as ash, beech or elm, set the right tone, as does linoleum, which is highly practical, 100 per cent natural and was a much-favoured flooring option until the mid-twentieth century. For a more comfortable alternative, fitted wool carpet throughout looks sleek, but choose a pale, understated colour. For those who prefer rugs, plain sisal mats, woollen rugs with abstract motifs, or even – for a cheeky nod to the Seventies – a wool shag-pile rug, all set a convincing retro tone.

BUILT-IN FURNITURE

In the drive towards a streamlined, modern look – and in revolt against the clumsier bulky furniture of the nineteenth century – there was a definitive trend in the middle of the twentieth century towards built-in storage. The Fifties, for example, saw the advent of the fitted kitchen. The streamlined kitchen is still with us today, but in the natural retro home consider having a fitted kitchen made from pure, unadulterated materials such as solid wood, rather than from the more unhealthy chipboard or MDF (see page 31).

ABOVE LEFT Twentieth-century classic furniture often boasts curvaceous lines. Use a neutral colour scheme, like the white walls and wood floor in this New York loft, to highlight your special pieces.

ABOVE Not all retro furniture needs to be teamed with wood surfaces. In this room, an Eero Saarinen table and Charles and Ray Eames chairs are set off against a Japanese blue slate floor.

OPPOSITE LEFT To show off a collection of classic furniture to its best advantage, keep upholstery and timber colours in similar tones. In this 1930s house, neutrals give a pulled-together look.

OPPOSITE RIGHT Curvy retro furniture looks best when there is space around it. The arrangement in this light-filled room is particularly successful.

Alternatively, for a truly retro look, source and recycle original mid-twentieth century kitchen units.

It's a bonus that built-in storage was a feature of the vintage home as everyone can do with bespoke cupboards. Yes, they are expensive, but great storage can transform a busy household and helps to maintain that coveted streamlined look. Talk to a joiner with a 'green' bent to find out the best materials to use. If solid wood is prohibitively expensive, consider the option of using formaldehyde-free MDF, which may be painted or combined with wood veneers. The latter give a beautiful, natural look and – although they will contain some glues – are an acceptable compromise for the natural retro home.

FREESTANDING FURNITURE

For some, the whole point of choosing a natural retro look is to showcase a collection of vintage furniture.

Whether you buy pieces for investment, for the purity of their design or for the romance of choosing modern-day antiques, ensuring the furniture fits your natural home ethos is crucial. Research favourite designers before buying and learn about their preferred materials. The Scandinavian Modern designers were particularly keen on using timber, especially rosewood, teak, walnut and mahogany, while the Modernists loved plywood and leather. Choosing vintage pieces is one way to have the rare hardwoods that are today considered less eco-sound. Fifties designers in particular favoured streamlined yet organic shapes, so hunt out long, leather sofas, easy chairs with spindly legs, lean, slim sideboards and curvy coffee tables, all of which team well with modern pieces. And remember that it's not vital to stick to big-name designers: an original black leather and rosewood Charles and Ray Eames' lounge chair will have a sky-high price tag.

FABRICS

Understated yet sculptural window treatments are the most appropriate choices for the natural retro home, particularly at large picture windows. The Modernists favoured very simple curtains hanging loose from slim wooden poles and in plain but textural fabrics. Linen, hemp and heavy cotton are good choices and are robust enough to hang well and stay in crisp folds. Curtain poles may be wood or leather-covered. Upholstery choices should also be understated. The Modernists favoured fitted over loose covers, so consider strong, tactile materials like leather, linen, wool and cotton that highlight the curvy shapes of the period furniture.

The Fifties in particular was also a time of experimentation in printed textiles. Notable designers such as Lucien Day, for example, created dynamic abstract designs, influenced by the natural world. To re-create a similar look, either hunt down original vintage fabrics, or source modern-day reproductions: some of Day's designs, for example, can now be digitally reproduced on cotton. A dash of pattern, amidst the vintage furniture, will create vital contrast.

COLOUR

When creating a retro look, it's not essential to slavishly copy original colour schemes: instead, loosely interpret tones that might have been popular earlier in the twentieth century. Both the Modernists and the Scandinavian Moderns favoured white walls, often with upholstery in muted shades such as oatmeal, pale grey or black. Yet the Fifties also brought with it a more light-hearted obsession with colour, from bubble-gum pinks to unusual tones like acid yellow and turquoise. Used sparingly, these create wonderful accent shades.

TAKE A RETRO MOOD AS YOUR STARTING POINT, RATHER THAN AS AN END IN ITSELF. USE SPARE LINES AND NATURAL MATERIALS TO CREATE YOUR INDIVIDUAL SPIN ON VINTAGE STYLE

THIS PAGE The Modernists favoured muted, toned-down colours, so compose a subtle colour scheme to show off the furniture to its best advantage. Here, pale stone and cream colours work well.

OPPOSITE Bold, graphic prints were a feature of the 1950s in particular. Using just one wall hanging or a curtain is enough to create an authentic vintage mood, especially when teamed with some classic pieces of furniture.

THIS PAGE Although wooden floors are the healthiest option because they don't trap dust or harbour dust mites as carpets do, it can be a good idea in a sitting room to add a soft natural fibre rug on top of the boards. The sheen of the boards, and the nubbly texture of the fibres create an interesting contrast.

- To lighten softwood floorboards, use Swedish lye, designed to take the yellow out of pine. After treatment, oil the boards. To enhance a bleached finish, clean with white Swedish soap.

- Don't rush to correct every tiny speck of damage. The beauty of a wood floor is that, over time, it develops its own unique patina.

- Some wooden floor-maintenance products contain waxes and essential oils, which will repair minor scratches and marks.

Maintaining a wooden floor

The most natural finish for a wooden floor is oil or oil and wax, either of which imparts a soft sheen, unlike the high gloss of acrylic lacquer or varnish. For everyday care, floorboards should be vacuumed to remove dust, then washed with a damp mop. Every six months, treat the boards with natural floor oil, followed by a thin coat of wax for a more hard-wearing finish. To treat any small patches of damage, rub the area with wire wool or fine sandpaper, then re-apply the oil and wax. There are many natural floor cleaners on the market, ranging from plant soaps to cleaners that contain natural vegetable oils, so experiment to find the most effective for your floor. If you have a painted wooden floor, look for a gentle all-purpose cleaner to remove any grime, grease and dust.

ABOVE Unless badly damaged, keep the existing floorboards in a period property and simply sand them, then oil and wax. If replacements are needed, choose recycled boards for a similar look.

RIGHT Pure white painted floorboards look great in a bedroom. A daily mop will stop them getting dirty.

NATURAL DECORATIVE

The vogue for the whimsical is not for the faint-hearted but it is very glamorous. For those who are attracted to mixing patterns and colour and sophistication with eccentricity, Natural Decorative is the perfect look. It also blends easily with natural principles. Quirky recycled pieces of furniture are essential (and they tick the eco box) while beautiful natural fabrics like silk, and handicrafts such as embroidery, also get a chance to shine.

PATTERN

Pattern is the ultimate ingredient for the Natural Decorative look, especially bold designs featuring organic shapes or stylised botanical motifs. It isn't the quantity of pattern used that matters so much as the exuberance of the motif:

BELOW LEFT Despite its modern architecture and natural materials, which include slate floor slabs and Douglas-fir cladding, this Californian home benefits from a bold, patterned wall hanging to add a touch of individuality and decoration.

BELOW Give due consideration to where, and on what, you add pattern. The very delicacy of this antique sheer painted voile adds character, especially when hung close to the curvaceous mirror.

THIS PAGE A plain room, decked out in timber floors, white walls and neutral sofas, is transformed by the addition of a vibrantly decorative cushion combined with a circular Empire table and a pair of nineteenth-century chairs.

THIS PAGE A few carefully chosen, glittery accessories – such as the chandelier and decorative mirror here add glamour to the neutral tones, timber detailing and vintage furniture of this drawing room.

OPPOSITE Unusual and tactile textures will lift a neutral, classic scheme. In this London home, feathered headdresses from the Cameroons and velvet cushions add exoticism to the linens and woods elsewhere.

a sofa might be upholstered in a bold hand-blocked linen or a room simply accessorised with a single cushion featuring a giant appliqué. If you are choosing new fabrics, pay attention to their production. Many printed textiles use synthetic, non-environmentally friendly dyes, while dyeing consumes large quantities of water. Look for companies that are committed to producing vegetable-dyed fabrics, or textiles whose dyes are credited as being environmentally acceptable. Hand-embroidered motifs and vintage textiles are an alternative way to introduce pattern.

Patterned wallpaper looks dramatic used for a feature wall or as a detail, perhaps behind shelves. One ethically sound option is to source vintage wallpaper from a specialist supplier. Alternatively, find a wallpaper manufacturer committed to using 100 per

cent recycled papers and water-based dyes. Some producers are now turning to greener practices.

COLOUR

Colour is fundamental to the Natural Decorative home. For the necessary flamboyance, choose a palette of delicate sugared-almond shades or the shock of deeper jewel shades. It's also possible to tread a middle path, mixing one or two key accent colours, such as raspberry or indigo, with white and neutrals. Many organic paints come in a wide range of colours, or if you are using fabric to introduce colour, opt for textiles in softer shades that have been vegetable-dyed. Accessories, ranging from a wildly coloured piece of modern art to a hand-painted tabletop, are another way to introduce a vibrant mix of colour.

FURNITURE

Half the fun of the Natural Decorative look lies in combining whimsical or highly decorative pieces of furniture. Look in junk shops or vintage stores for pieces with curvy lines and romantic detailing, including carving, or seek out unusual natural inlays or trims, from shagreen (a rough leather, often made from stingray skin and usually dyed green) to mother-of-pearl. Precisely because you are recycling old pieces, you need have no worries about plundering the natural world for these exotic surfaces. Furniture can either be painted, made from exotic woods such as bird's eye maple or walnut, or from elaborately grained stone, such as a pink marble-topped wash stand. Vintage furniture with gently distressed gilding or the sparkle of mirror will add essential glamour.

OPPOSITE LEFT Just one dramatic, curvy piece of furniture can be enough to raise the tone from country to decorative. Here, a capacious antique wingchair does the trick.

OPPOSITE RIGHT A natural colour scheme will gain drama and character if it is mixed with a few jewel shades or even with a touch of gilding. In this bedroom, the gilded scarlet period bed adds a dash of glamour.

RIGHT Perhaps it is pattern, more than anything else, that adds a decorative flavour. In this exotic outdoor room, the natural materials of the awning are cleverly balanced by a bold pattern on the floor and armchair.

DECORATIVE TOUCHES

Given the exotic emphasis, it's fun to amass a choice of trimmings and accessories to complement the Natural Decorative look. Pheasant or peacock feathers, for example – in their natural state, rather than the dyed variety – create fabulously decadent trimmings for cushions or around a lampshade. Rabbit fur also makes a glamorous trimming, although its use can be contentious. While many suppliers justify selling the fur as 'a by-product of the rabbit-meat industry', many rabbits are still bred specifically for their pelts, which is an unsettling concept. Specialist shops are also good hunting grounds for sparkly chic accessories. Examples might include mother-of-pearl (from farmed sources) fashioned into dishes or table accessories, or shell spoons or dishes, carved from reclaimed shells.

- Glass shelves can be edged with tiny LED light fittings to illuminate and highlight a special display.

- In a family home, get the children to help create seasonal displays, such as nuts and seeds in autumn or seashells in summer.

- Flowers, leaves and grasses, simply arranged in slim glass vases or even in tumblers in a row, make the ultimate fresh and simple natural display for a mantelpiece or dining table.

Natural displays

The secret to a truly effective natural display lies not just in the objects, but in the confident way they are grouped together. A giant glass vase filled with tiny white pebbles can be as arresting as a wall of glass display cabinets filled with an old collection of exotic butterflies. Tactile objects like shells are often best displayed in a place where they can be touched - on a console table, for example, or beside a bath. Fragile treasures, such as ostrich eggs, feathers or fossils, look wonderful on narrow glass shelves or in a shallow bowl. One special single piece, perhaps on a mantelpiece, is also very eye-catching. The architectural style of the room doesn't matter, though many natural finds have a sculptural quality that often looks amazing in a spare, modern setting.

ABOVE AND RIGHT Exotic treasures, from animal bones to ostrich eggs and from tropical corals to seashells, can add a sense of whimsy to an interior.

OPPOSITE In a kitchen with understated walls and furniture, the spotlight is cast on the intriguing mix of stuffed animals and fish on the walls.

INSPIRATION SHOULD COME FROM VISUAL PROMPTS – THE LOOK OF THE SEA AND COUNTRYSIDE AROUND US – AS WELL AS THE NATURAL PHYSICAL MATERIALS AT OUR DISPOSAL

NATURAL COASTAL

Whether a seaside property is your permanent home or a bolt hole for high days and holidays, it should always have an alluring, relaxing appeal. The decorative style you use should be comfortable and timeless, offering the vital sense of freshness and simplicity that we all long for while on vacation. We can't all have a beachfront house or even a sea view, but use the elemental features of water, sand and rocks as your visual inspiration for a Natural Coastal style. Of all the key decorative styles you might choose from, this is one of the easiest to copy and is the simplest to interpret using natural materials.

SURFACES

Think of the seaside, and weathered, sun-bleached materials instantly come to mind. Take inspiration from the smooth, worn texture and pale colours of a piece of driftwood, or the weather-beaten hull of a painted rowing boat, and try to re-create that mood with appropriate worktops and flooring. Old floorboards can be sanded and limed, using natural Scandinavian white soap or, if you are buying new, invest in narrow ash or beech ship-style decking, treated with a simple natural oiled finish to bring out the grain of the wood. Walls – and even ceilings – can be panelled with wooden tongue-and-groove boards, then painted with organic paints in either white or in pale shades of blue or grey.

Certain stone surfaces are particularly appropriate by the seaside. Some limestone varieties, for example, have the natural indentations of tiny shell fossils, and their pale yellow colour is reminiscent of sandy shores.

THIS PAGE Use nautical inspirations for a seaside theme. In this Long Island waterside home, painted wooden boards and plenty of white create a relaxed, summer-time mood.

OPPOSITE Just as the coast combines a mix of contrasting textures, from smooth pebbles to rough sand, so too should the Natural Coastal home. Mix painted wooden boards with rough basketwork, raffia and coarse linens.

Alternatively, if the seaside home is closer to craggy rocks, then a grey riven slate might be more appropriate, perhaps used for flooring, or choose a grey or grey-green flecked granite for a kitchen worktop. Keep finishes matt or honed rather than glossy. For bathroom floors, choose bamboo flooring or natural cork, both of which are superb eco choices, look very textural, and are particularly waterproof.

COLOUR

Colour is a vital tool when creating a seaside mood. Experiment with sample pots of varied blues and aquas, or ask an organic paint company to mix a shade exactly to your specification, using a photo of the sea as inspiration. It's not essential to stick to the blue spectrum, though. Coastal style can veer towards a variety of pale and dark greys ranging from seagull white to graphite, towards a palette of softer colours like sand or terracotta, or towards the pinks, from the coral of a sunset to palest shell. For those in search of

bright colours, take inspiration from striped beach huts in colours that run the gamut from scarlet to emerald, or be inspired by the bright tones of classic cotton canvas striped deck-chair fabric.

FABRICS

Look for a mix of tough, plain fabrics such as cotton canvas, madras cotton and denim. A sofa, for example, might be upholstered in blue denim with cushions in striped blue-and-white ticking, or a headboard could be covered in heavy hopsack linen and teamed with antique linen sheets. If possible, pick loose covers over upholstery, so that they are washable and easy to maintain. Try cotton towelling on a bathroom chair, or natural cotton duck, which is a durable, close-woven

OPPOSITE Scan the neutral spectrum for appropriate colours in the coastal home. Pale, bleached tones are an excellent foil to the blue of the sea and sky outside.

OPPOSITE BELOW LEFT Stripes, especially in blue and white or in candy deck-chair colours, are the perfect decorative shorthand in the Natural Coastal home. Choose tough striped cotton to update a junk-shop chair.

RIGHT A casual, eclectic mix of crunchy textiles creates the right mood on a bed. Look for hand-loomed throws and light wool blankets, plus organic cotton bedlinen.

heavy cotton, for an armchair. Choose tablecloths made from vegetable-dyed antique linen sheets, napkins made from vintage linen tea-towel fabric, or a table runner stitched in 100 per cent cotton deck-chair fabric.

When it comes to fabrics for window treatments, think unlined and floaty to catch the sea breeze and prettily filter the light while giving tantalising glimpses of a great view. Good choices are ruched butter muslin, hemp and fine, crunchy linen or cotton voile. Plains look good by the sea, but so do checks and sun-bleached florals, as well as stripes in every width. Fabrics should be easy to wash: Natural Coastal is not the place for silk, wool or delicate embroidery.

Window treatments should be simple and easy. Plain curtains with a gathered heading, tab-top or slot-heading drapes, or fabric panels with eyelets strung onto a pole with jute string, all look appropriate. Choose a slim wood or bamboo curtain pole or try a strong leather thong, stretched tight, which is perfect for the finest of voile curtains. Some companies specialise in curtain poles with finials featuring shell or pebble detailing, and it's also possible to buy curtain clips decorated with real, reclaimed, shells. Blinds should be Roman or simple roll-up styles in gauzy linen or plain cotton. Wooden Venetian blinds, in dark or light stains, or American-style shutters, are another good option. And don't forget trimmings and details. A blind pull featuring a pebble, or tiny shells stitched onto the leading edge of a canvas curtain, all look extremely pretty and underline the coastal mood.

LEFT The Natural Coastal home is not the place for sleek, fitted furniture. Instead, freestanding easy pieces, either in painted wood or bespoke one-offs fashioned from driftwood, are the best choices.

OPPOSITE Painting junk-shop furniture not only unifies different pieces and gives a cohesive look, but offers the chance to introduce a seaside mood, using a palette of soft blues, lilac or pale grey.

FURNITURE

Natural Coastal style should combine lightness of touch with a sense of comfort. The scrubbed, easy-going mood cries out for junk-style furniture, from a calico loose-covered armchair trimmed with abalone or coconut-shell buttons, to old church pews for casual dining-room seating. Think about the kitchen. This is not the place for gleaming wooden cabinets and sleek smooth surfaces. Instead, consider putting together a relaxed cooking zone using unfitted pieces: a scrubbed pine table in the centre of the room, an open dresser and a length of recycled marble as a kitchen worktop, perhaps teamed with a second-hand butler's sink.

Sofas and armchairs should be squashy, and beds casually dressed. This might be the ideal time to invest in a simple, perhaps painted, wood-framed four-poster bed hung with muslin curtains, or a chaise longue covered in soft, unbleached organic cotton and placed in a relaxing bathroom. Bathroom fittings should be kept simple. A vintage armoire, its door panels covered in chicken wire or with gathered cotton fabric panels, is the perfect place to store towels, while a freestanding wooden towel rail looks more appropriate than the slick steel wall-mounted variety.

Do also consider driftwood furniture for the Natural Coastal home. A single bench, mirror or coffee table made from driftwood can be enough to create the right mood. Seek out specialist craftsmen and artists — many of whom live by the sea — who will make furniture to order. The appeal of such pieces is that every piece of driftwood is different, each has a varied patina and every stick of furniture will be unique.

Restoring old furniture

- Sagging upholstered furniture can be given a new lease of life with fresh seat cushions. Use traditional webbing and feather cushions, and always avoid foam fillings.

- Tired leather upholstery benefits from regular cleaning with saddle soap followed by a buffing. Use a specialist cleaner to treat small stains.

- Old wood furniture should be polished every six months with beeswax on a soft cloth.

It is often the ageing process that adds to the charm of an old piece of furniture, yet a little gentle renovation won't go amiss either. When buying vintage pieces, bear in mind that there's no point snapping up a bargain only to spend a fortune repairing it. Though minor touching up can be done at home, major repairs on good antique furniture should always be done by a specialist. Some wood just needs the encrusted wax polish removed. Try methylated spirit on fine-grade wire wool, then finish with beeswax polish and buff well. Small scratches can be concealed using a specialist wood-dye pen or experiment with matching shoe polish. Tiny holes or dents may be filled using a small quantity of coloured wax, melted into the hole, then buffed with polish.

ABOVE AND RIGHT A mix of old painted furniture and scrubbed pine works well in a kitchen, as everyday scuffs and marks won't be too obvious.

OPPOSITE Employ a good carpenter for simple furniture repairs. Old furniture shouldn't look too pristine, so gently 'distress' new paint using wire wool.

Natural Surfaces, Fabrics and Colour

THIS PAGE A neutral colour scheme, teamed with reclaimed timber beams and an eighteenth-century French stone fireplace, create all the right elements for a warm, relaxing natural home in a converted stable.

The materials we choose to create the look, feel, mood and substance of our homes are of vital importance. In the natural home, where we are concerned with our health and that of the planet, those materials take on even greater significance.

Crystallising our thoughts on the style we want to achieve provides valuable pointers to the materials needed, but that's just the start. Within each category there are myriad choices. It pays to ask searching questions about the origins and production of each material, but there are also financial and ethical compromises. Thus, there is no doubt that it's expensive to deck out a home in natural surfaces. But if, for instance, you can't afford an entire bathroom in marble, you could invest instead in one modest slab as a bath splashback.

Tricky ethical questions need honest answers, too. Laying a bamboo floor is perfectly 'green', for example, but what price the carbon footprint when that flooring has to be transported from far-off shores?

Visit plenty of showrooms, quarries or suppliers: touch, examine, compare and contrast varied materials, perhaps even build up a sample board. Ask questions about the care of the materials and their ageing process. After all, the joy of natural surfaces is that they get better as they mature: think of the softening of linens or the beautiful patina on wood. The investment you make now will reap benefits far into the future.

OPPOSITE ABOVE LEFT Cool, robust, and packed with visual nuances, stone makes a good-looking and hard-wearing choice anywhere in the house.

OPPOSITE ABOVE RIGHT Newly installed or a period feature, an age-worn timber staircase not only looks beautiful, but feels wonderful underfoot.

OPPOSITE CENTRE LEFT Cotton, linen and hemp are the most natural of fabrics, and are also light, strong and breathable.

OPPOSITE CENTRE RIGHT Vintage natural fabrics, often with decorative detailing, are worth hunting out and may be 'repurposed' in many ways.

OPPOSITE BELOW LEFT Unfussy treatments show off natural textural fabrics to their best advantage and keep them looking chic.

OPPOSITE BELOW RIGHT Look for beautiful detailing, whether in the loose strands of a silk and cotton Moroccan shawl, in the fossils embedded in a piece of stone or in the rich grain of timber.

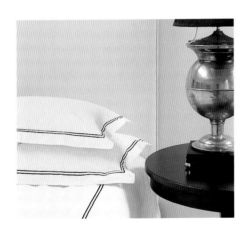

OPPOSITE ABOVE LEFT Chunky masonry needn't be reserved only for rustic interiors. In this chic, modern bathroom, a stone feature panel enhances the crispness of the fittings.

OPPOSITE ABOVE RIGHT Original stonework in older properties should be carefully repaired by a specialist, as was the case in this rustic outbuilding.

OPPOSITE BELOW LEFT In a new-build property with a mezzanine floor, recycled local stone teamed with timber planking adds a cosy, tactile mood to an essentially modern room.

OPPOSITE BELOW RIGHT Stone-clad walls produce strong patterns. Here, intricate stones are calmed by simple, clean-lined furniture.

HARD SURFACES

ABOVE The use of stone requires a careful blending of textures. In this rustic dining room, the rough walls are balanced by the smoothness of the timber beams and the richness of the grain in the chairs.

MASONRY STONE

Visually and emotionally, a stone-built or stone-clad wall is a fast-track way to create a natural look. Whether used as block stone or as irregularly cut pieces set into mortar, stone instantly brings to mind the natural world outside. Yet it is also an extremely durable and low-maintenance choice at home. There is a vast choice of shapes, sizes and textures, and rubble masonry can be used for walls, floors or arches. Stylistically, pick the tone and shape of stones to fit the architecture: a regular block stone may suit a modern city flat, whereas irregular pieces will sit well in a rural home. Stone must be quarried, so while it is a natural choice, there is inevitably an environmental impact. You can reduce this by choosing local quarried stone, or by using reclaimed materials from a nearby building. Each regional stone will have its own special colour and texture so ensure it fits into your planned scheme.

SLAB STONE

Cut from the earth, durable slab stone is the ultimate natural resource. Today it has become an incredibly popular surface in our homes, and – sold by the square metre/yard or in tile form – can be used for flooring, worktops, splashbacks and as wall tiling. Some stone is porous so must be properly sealed: get specialist advice from your supplier. The most common types include marble, limestone, travertine, granite and slate. By all means pick stone for the beauty of its colours and markings, but also double-check with the supplier as to its suitability for your intended use. You also need to consider which finish – highly polished, honed or textured – will best suit your chosen style.

Marble, limestone and travertine

These three types of stone all started out as sediment that, over millions of years, solidified into stone. Highly polished marble has elegant veining and comes in an irresistible choice of colours from delicate white or pink to black or dark green. Limestone comes in paler shades, from buttermilk to soft yellow, and often contains tiny fossils or shells, while naturally pitted travertine, which comes in delicious caramel, burnt orange or creamy shades, is often filled before being polished or honed.

Granite

Granite is formed when molten rock is forced between other rocks in the Earth's crust. As it cools, it solidifies into a granular, crystalline structure. It has a characteristic flecked appearance and comes in dark shades ranging from grey and black to rich browns. It's a hard stone, perfect for kitchens because it is resistant to household acids.

Slate

Formed in ancient river beds where particles washed downstream are pressed together into layers, slate boasts a rippled, uneven surface with strongly rustic properties. Colours vary from palest grey to dense black, moss green and silver blue.

NATURAL SURFACES ARE BEAUTIFUL, ENDURING AND TACTILE. TAKE TIME TO SELECT STONE IN A COLOUR, TEXTURE AND FINISH THAT WILL SUIT YOUR LIFESTYLE AND PLEASE THE EYE

THIS PAGE As well as being used for floors or worktops, look out for beautiful veined marble on furniture. A marble-topped French farmhouse table, such as this one, adds practicality and beauty to a kitchen in New York.

OPPOSITE When selecting stone slabs for flooring, take time to choose not just the colour and texture, but how the geometry of the joint lines will work. Giant slabs in a small room, for example, can make the room look larger.

PLASTER FINISHES

If you want a textured wall finish, try to avoid cement finishes or cement-based plasters. Cement is harmful to the environment: in fact, its manufacturing process ranks it third in the world in the production of CO_2 emissions after energy generation and transport. Traditional lime plaster offers an attractive, natural alternative. This contains lime putty, sand, chalk and hair, and – although it takes longer to dry than cement – it is healthier for the world (and your home). Incredibly durable, it feels warmer to the touch than cement and has a rich pink-brown colour. Clay plasters are an alternative to lime plaster. Made from fine sand and clay, usually with no added pigment, they create a natural, warm-toned finish and, as they require little processing, are very environmentally friendly.

ABOVE Plaster-based wall finishes create a useful link between natural, rustic architectural features and a slick modern style. In this Italian home, furniture and lighting are crisp and simple in contrast with a textural wall.

RIGHT It's important to balance textural surfaces with smooth details. In this New York apartment, the sheen of the wooden furniture and the glass of the window provide a foil to the irregularity of the walls.

THIS PAGE Here plaster walls have been coloured pale yellow by injecting pigment and water to give a warm, yet gently distressed finish. Native pottery, natural fabric upholstery and wood are the finishing touches in this contemporary country interior.

THIS PAGE Wood with a well-defined grain, used on walls as panels, can add as strong a pattern as wallpaper. In this Parisian bedroom, the enveloping effect of the panels creates a cosy sleeping nook.

OPPOSITE Timber wall panelling can create many different effects. In this room, the subtle horizontal grain of southern yellow pine tongue-and-groove, teamed with a Charles and Ray Eames screen, creates a sleek modern look.

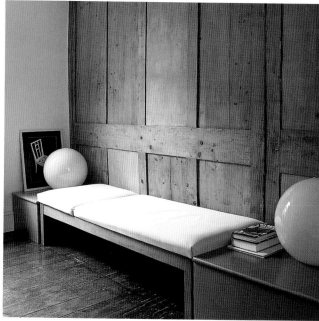

TIMBER

Ultra-durable, beautiful to look at and warm to the touch, wood is essential in the natural home. Yet using timber comes at an ethical price. We all know that the destruction of the world's forests has contributed to global warming, so all new timber should be accredited by the Forest Stewardship Council (FSC), which is an international non-governmental organisation that promotes good forest management. If possible, purchase wood from local sources, which reduces the distance the timber has to travel and, hence, its carbon footprint. Buying locally sourced wood, however, inevitably rules out the more exotic woods such as African mahogany and wenge.

Timber flooring

Ideally, a new wood floor should be of solid wood. Engineered wood floors, which are cheaper, consist of several wood plies glued together. If using these, check whether the glue is low-VOC (see page 31). Laminate flooring is best avoided as it consists of a layer of décor paper under a protective film, all glued and pressed onto high-density backing board. Whether a wood floor looks sophisticated or rustic is down to the knotting and grain, the width of

ABOVE LEFT Dark, heavily grained wooden walls and floors create a very moody interior. Include pale accent colours and softer textures for balance.

ABOVE Traditional period wood panelling can look simple or highly decorative, depending on the style of the panels used.

OPPOSITE LEFT Tongue-and-groove wood panelling painted in a pale colour can create a classic, elegant background. Here, it is a perfect foil to the decorative Arts and Crafts table and chairs.

OPPOSITE RIGHT A reclaimed wooden floor has a gently worn patina that is perfect for a period property as in this Provençal house, rebuilt using reclaimed chestnut floorboards.

the boards and the finish of the wood. Natural wood oils and wood soaps bring out the beauty of the grain and protect the wood.

Wooden worktops

Whether for kitchens or bathrooms, wooden worktops are durable, waterproof and improve with age, but they must be looked after appropriately. Apply oil regularly and be sure to clean up any stains as quickly as possible.

Wood panelling

Wood makes handsome wall panels and looks dramatic on ceilings, too. Wide panels of solid wood or wood veneer – which makes good sustainable sense because far less wood is used – suit a modern setting best. In a period country property, where a more textural look is appropriate, choose solid wood panels. Hire a specialist joiner to create panelling to match existing features, or consider using salvaged panels. For a very simple property, softwood tongue-and-groove cladding can be stained or painted, and is comparatively inexpensive.

LINO, CORK AND BAMBOO

Lino and cork are back in fashion. Lino, made from wood, flour, pine resin, linseed oil and natural pigment, is recyclable and non-toxic. It's also warm, durable, comes in lots of colours and is perfect for bathrooms, kitchens and children's rooms. Cork is inexpensive and comes either in its natural honey colour or stained. Finish it with natural wax rather than shiny varnish. Bamboo flooring is one of the most renewable and abundant natural resources. To make it, strips of solid bamboo are engineered into several layers, using low-VOC adhesive. The resulting floors are very durable.

SOFT SURFACES

LEATHER

Leather is pliable to the touch, hard-wearing, ages to a wonderful patina and can be successfully used for floors, wall panelling and upholstery. It's not a cheap option, though, and it also raises a number of ecological and ethical questions: the curing, tanning and dyeing process uses a great deal of water, and it's important to seek out leathers that, like fabrics, use low-impact dyes. Some people also query whether categorising leather as a by-product of the food industry is enough to justify the use of animal skins.

When buying leather, check its suitability by type. Aniline leather is the most natural-looking but it soils easily. Semi-aniline leather has a light surface coating, while pigmented leather has a full protective coating.

BELOW LEFT A successful interior combines good-looking furniture and surfaces with a mix of textures. Here, worn timber sits alongside crisp fabric upholstery and textural natural flooring.

BELOW Even a very sophisticated interior will benefit from a clever combination of varied surfaces. In this chic neutral scheme, glamour is achieved by mixing wool carpet with linen upholstery, as well as with leather and cowhide.

OPPOSITE Supple yet hard-wearing, leather can be used to upholster walls as well as for floors. In this eclectically decorated bedroom, warm ginger leather squares cover the walls, with a modern striped wool carpet for contrast.

THIS PAGE Natural fibre flooring, be it sisal, coir or medieval matting, provides a highly decorative and very satisfying alternative to wool carpet. In this elegant yet rustic drawing room, the matting adds softness to a timber floor.

OPPOSITE LEFT Animal skins offer a dramatic and highly textural way to decorate and accessorise a room. In this London townhouse, a zebra rug and stripped buffalo skin rugs add pattern to an otherwise serene interior.

OPPOSITE RIGHT Natural fibre options are usually available as fitted wall-to-wall flooring or cut to order into rugs, bound either in a neutral or in a contrast colour. Varied decorative effects can be achieved by choosing either a smooth or a rough-textured, weave.

Animal hides

The more exotic animal hides, whether used for beanbags, cushions or rugs, add interest and texture to a room. Specialist suppliers offer tactile options such as rabbit fur, organic sheepskin or eel-skin cushions, as well as Mongolian lamb, zebra print and cowhide rugs.

NATURAL-FIBRE FLOORING

One hundred per cent natural-fibre flooring is a great alternative to carpet. It feels rougher and doesn't clean so effectively, but it looks very smart. Most types can be cut into rugs, laid like carpet or used as stair runners.

Seagrass

Seagrass is a strong, naturally stain-resistant fibre. It cannot be dyed, but comes in a surprisingly wide variety of tones and colours.

Coir

Coir is a coarse fibre, originating from the coconut. It is one of the cheapest natural floorings, comes in a variety of weaves and is very hard-wearing.

Sisal

Sisal comes from a bush that is similar to the yucca plant. Traditionally used to make rope, it is naturally strong and as it holds colour well, it can be dyed to many shades. Available in a number of weaves and designs, it is a particularly sophisticated flooring choice.

Jute

This is the finest and softest of all the natural fibres, and so is most appropriate for areas of light traffic.

WOOL CARPET

Wool carpet is soft and durable, has natural insulating properties and an inbuilt resistance to soiling. It's also possible to get wool carpet mixed with natural fibres such as sisal, or with luxury fibres like linen or silk. In the natural home, avoid wool carpets blended with nylon and polyester. Also try and avoid carpets with a plastic backing, which means they aren't biodegradable. The natural alternative is to seek out a carpet with a jute backing, and to opt for a traditional felt, hessian or natural latex rubber underlay, rather than foam.

LUXURY FABRICS

The classic luxury fabrics, such as linen, hemp, silk, wool and horsehair, are among the most elegant-looking of textiles so you'll find that it's perfectly possible to go natural and still create a glamorous finish for the home.

LINEN

Linen is a fine, strong fabric made from flax. Its use dates back to Egyptian times. It has a natural crispness and lustre, and gently softens with each wash. Weaves vary from coarse to fine, so there's a linen type appropriate for upholstery, table and bedlinens, and window treatments. Look out for natural, undyed varieties or vegetable-dyed linens. Antique linen sheets are an environmentally sound option, too.

HEMP

Hemp derives from the hemp plant (part of the cannabis family) and is a strong fibre, yet very soft once woven. Less water is used in the production of hemp than for cotton or linen, therefore it is particularly 'green'. Many organic specialist suppliers offer hemp bedlinen, tablelinen and fabric by the metre/yard.

SILK

The raw silk thread made from the cocoon of the silkworm is the basis of all silk yarns. It's available in a multitude of types and weights, from fine habotai to wild silk, and can be plain, two-tone or decorated with hand-blocked designs. For interior use, silk is best reserved for cushions or light upholstery.

WOOL

Dense, comforting and with fantastic insulating properties, 100 per cent wool fabrics are brilliant for upholstery or curtains. Wool mixes with linen, cotton or silk offer a lighter-weight alternative. Look for locally produced, organic wool from specialist companies. The soft, strong yarn from the alpaca, in a range of natural colours, is another 'green' alternative.

HORSEHAIR

Horsehair is sourced from live horses and is woven with a cotton warp. It is an expensive but high-quality upholstery fabric, available from specialist suppliers, and comes in plain colours and smart stripes with a glossy sheen.

OPPOSITE ABOVE LEFT
A beautifully textured fine fabric, such as linen or wool, can be enhanced by excellent soft-furnishing design. In this elegant dining room, skirted chair covers show off crisp fabric choices.

OPPOSITE ABOVE RIGHT
Cream or neutral linen curtains are very sophisticated, especially when the linen falls in strong sculptural folds. These curtains are made from old linen sheets from a convent.

OPPOSITE BELOW LEFT
Linen, hemp and wool all make excellent upholstery choices. In this smart dining room, buttoning adds a new dimension to an already textural fabric.

OPPOSITE BELOW RIGHT
If a beautiful fabric is expensive, it's always possible to use just a small amount for a cushion or a throw. Plain detailing, such as simple piping or pin-tucking, will enhance an attractive sheen or weave.

UTILITY FABRICS

The so-called utility fabrics, such as cotton, ticking, canvas, muslin and hessian, are made from natural fibres and are traditionally hard-wearing and good value for money. They look fantastic in a Natural Country interior but are equally at home as part of a modern scheme. In a decorative interior, experiment by mixing them with exotic trimmings like horn or leather buttons, or team with vibrant, hand-blocked textiles.

COTTON

Cotton comes in a huge variety of weights and styles, from hand-loomed, vegetable-dyed Indian cottons, some of which are suitable for upholstery, to lightweight gingham and tough denim. Cotton production is responsible for a quarter of the world's pesticides, so look out for specialist suppliers who stock organic cotton, now farmed in many countries worldwide.

TICKING

Traditionally used for mattress coverings, ticking is a strong cotton cloth featuring crisp stripes, from narrow to wide, and has a timeless appeal. This functional fabric is perfect for upholstery, loose covers and window treatments. Look out for vintage ticking, gently softened by age.

CALICO AND COTTON CANVAS

These two cottons are staples of the utility fabric market. Calico is relatively lightweight and, in its unbleached state, features the dark specks of the cotton seed. It can be used for curtains or blinds. Cotton canvas comes in a variety of weights and is a tougher fabric suitable for upholstery or curtains.

HESSIAN AND JUTE SCRIM

Rough to the touch and a deep beige colour in their natural state, hessian and jute textiles are inexpensive but useful. Hessian is great for upholstery – and can look very sophisticated on an antique sofa – while jute scrim, with its light, open weave, is excellent for rustic-looking unlined curtains. Paper-backed hessian is a natural, decorative alternative for use on walls.

SHEER FABRICS

THIS PAGE A sheer neutral cotton, stitched into long, slim panels and simply hung from battens, can serve both to screen out harsh sunlight and to create a moody atmosphere in a relaxed sitting zone.

OPPOSITE For a dramatic floor-to-ceiling window treatment, it's worth seeking out sheer natural fabrics with unusual detailing. These glorious sheers, in a warm neutral, are made from locally woven raffia.

There are a multitude of beautiful sheer natural fabrics available, from the delicacy of fine, open-weave linens, to coloured muslins and hand-embroidered Indian cotton voiles. Sheers are vital in the natural home, to layer with curtains to control light or conceal a view, and to add texture and colour to a scheme. Most importantly, their presence is vital to soften hard surfaces such as stone and wood, and to add intricacy of detail and a sense of gentle movement in a room. Although most sheers come in white or delicate neutral colours, it's worth experimenting with deeper shades such as chocolate or grey to tone with stone or wood. Look for interesting details such as drawn thread-work, lace inset panels, a crunchy open weave or embroidery, all of which will be highlighted as the sun shines through the sheer. And remember that sheers don't just have to be used for simple curtains: they can look beautiful stitched into hanging panels or made into roll-up blinds.

SILK

Light, floaty silks – from taffetas to voile, organdie to habotai – are made from fine twisted yarn, loose-woven so the fabric is almost transparent. Silk sheers should be kept away from sunlight, so are best teamed with a plain cotton blind, or use them to make tie-on panels to surround a four-poster bed.

MUSLIN

Muslin, or butter muslin, is an incredibly fine fabric. In its unbleached state it is pale cream. Stitched into sheers with a narrow slot heading, generous lengths of it can be gathered onto a narrow wooden or bamboo pole so that it filters the sunlight. Even finer versions include muslin made from Egyptian cotton.

LINEN AND LINEN SCRIM

Look out for very lightweight, drapeable linens, either undyed or vegetable-dyed. These can be made up into easy unlined Roman blinds or hung with tie-tab headings from a slim curtain pole. Linen scrim in either white or natural is often available from fabric wholesalers. It has an open-mesh weave, which makes it the perfect sheer for a seaside setting.

EMBROIDERED SHEERS

Fairtrade suppliers are good sources of beautiful curtain panels that have been hand-embroidered by women working in co-operatives in developing countries. These embroidered panels are often made of sheer organic cottons, hemp or linen.

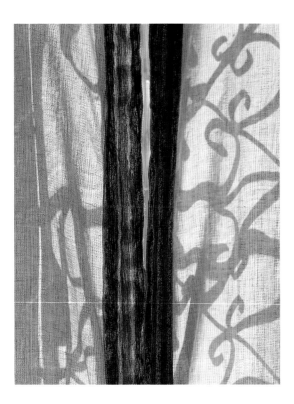
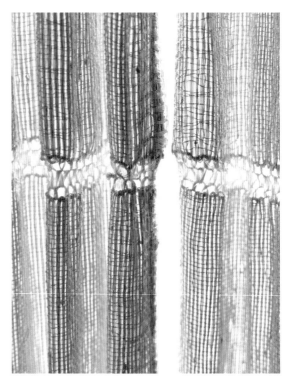

OPPOSITE BELOW LEFT
The beauty of a sheer natural fabric is that sunshine can gently filter through. This sheer cotton panel window treatment shows up the lovely silhouette of a decorative iron grille outside.

OPPOSITE BELOW RIGHT
It's worth hunting out specialist textile suppliers or looking at local textiles when travelling, to find unusual lengths of natural fabrics. This one is hand-woven raffia.

THIS PAGE Sheer fabrics can make fantastic Roman blinds, perfect for both screening and controlling sunlight. Keep them unlined and enjoy the play of sunshine on the light, open-weave textures.

THIS PAGE Organic bedlinen is one of the easiest ways to invest in organic textiles. Although some linens are unbleached and quite plain, others come with decorative embroidery or pin-tucking for a more sophisticated look.

OPPOSITE LEFT AND RIGHT Websites are good hunting grounds for beautiful, organic home accessories, such as alpaca cushions, hemp curtain panels or organic cotton tablelinens. Look out for unusual detailing, such as wood or shell buttons.

ORGANIC FABRICS

These days we're all urged to buy organic, from food to fabric, from skin-care products to cleaning products and from holidays to baby wear. The pressure is such that 'organic' can seem to be nothing more than the latest buzz word. It's important, therefore, to understand exactly what organic means in the context of fabrics for the home. Organic fabrics will have been created in ways that are kind to the earth (without the use of artificial chemicals or pesticides) and kind (i.e. not harmful) to humans.

HOME TEXTILES

Nowadays there is an increasing choice of organic textiles such as organic cotton, linen and hemp. Organic cotton fibres are sometimes more durable and softer than those grown with pesticides. Many organic textiles are available either in an undyed natural form, or are dyed using low-impact environmentally friendly dyes. As well as being available off the roll for home-sewing projects, they are also made up into tablecloths, runners, napkins, towels, tea-towels, bedlinen and curtains. They do not have the 'worthy' image you might imagine, either. You can choose from glamorous waffle-style towels to stylish tab-top curtain panels, to sophisticated drawn thread-work tablelinens.

Once you are committed to the principles of organic textiles, why not try other accessories? Silk-filled duvets and pillows, which are naturally hypo-allergenic, 100 per cent organic wool pillows and organic millet-seed pillows are all great natural additions to the bedroom. They feel wonderful, are ecologically sound and promote good health, too.

USING COLOUR

Think natural, and it is the pale, creamy tones that first come to mind, from off-white to buttermilk, followed by the stronger dark naturals, from the colours of the variegated grain of walnut through to the sombre tones of lava stone. For those in search of a neutral interior, that's all well and good, but if you long for colour, it's still possible to create a vibrant interior inspired by nature. You only have to look at the landscape on a sunny day to see luminous blues and berry reds, not to mention the paler mid-tones of lilac, salmon pink or lichen.

Whichever natural colour palette you opt for, it helps to put together a colour and sample board before finalising your decorative scheme. Wall and ceiling colours must be balanced with flooring, upholstery choices with window treatments, and you must not forget that natural materials, such as stone, wood and bamboo, all have their own inherent patterns and colours. Using such a board will help ensure you get the balance right.

EXPLORE COLOUR IN THE NATURAL WORLD, FROM THE DELICATE BLOOM OF A SHELL TO THE MYRIAD GREENERY OF VEGETATION. CHOOSING A COLOUR SCHEME THEN BECOMES EFFORTLESS

THIS PAGE In a period interior, keep to soft, subtle off-whites and team with limed wood or – in a seaside house – with one or two pieces of furniture made from driftwood. Organic paints offer a good selection of pale shades.

OPPOSITE ABOVE LEFT A pure white scheme can look very dramatic when contrasted with the rich, deep colour nuances of a natural floor, be that dark stained timber boards or a grey-green slate.

OPPOSITE BELOW RIGHT Scour paint charts for pale, bleached tones. In this tongue-and-groove panelled bathroom, the boards have been painted a soft dove grey to add sophistication.

LIGHT TONES

A pale colour palette feels tranquil, enhances small spaces and is easy to accessorise, but for a mellow look, forget about pure white, which can appear unnatural. Instead, scan paint charts, fabrics and found objects for true off-whites, from barley whites through to palest dove greys.

Varied texture adds interest to a bleached-out colour scheme. This is where the weave of a curtain fabric, the grain of wood or the veining of stone come into their own. For those wavering over which key neutral colour to pick, turn the process on its head. First, select an attractive piece of stone or bleached wood as the basis of your scheme, then pick out two or three pale tones from its subtle gradations of colour and pattern. Pale tones needn't be restricted to off-white, grey and cream: gentle duck-egg blue, shell pinks or warm mushroom all look fantastic, too.

Contrasting a pale scheme with a few well-selected darker elements also looks dramatic. The most obvious solution is to team pale walls and ceiling with a dark timber or warm terracotta floor. Or experiment and reverse the trend. A charcoal-painted ceiling, teamed with a few key pieces of worn, dark leather upholstery, with everything else in the room very pale, can look equally effective. Alternatively choose a natural, yet bright accent shade – leaf

BELOW LEFT In this country sitting room, the walls have been painted with chalk and natural pigment from the earth found around the property. The light, yet warm tones of the walls contrast well with the dramatic sculptural Chinese chair.

BELOW RIGHT When using off-whites, consider using a layered effect, with slightly varied tones of white on everything from walls and woodwork to upholstery and curtains. This country sitting room looks light and fresh.

OPPOSITE For a warm, cosy mood, stick to yellow-toned pale colours, from biscuit to ginger. This English sitting room moves tonally from the pale cream of the curtains to the mellow browns of the wooden beams and the leather chair.

green, perhaps, or scarlet – and use it sparingly in the piping on a cushion, or for upholstery on a single occasional chair to 'lift' a bleached-out scheme.

DARK TONES

Once you've trawled the myriad natural materials, it's easy to see that nature offers a truly inspiring palette of darker tones. Think, for example, of storm-cloud greys and bark browns with accents of plum or olive. A scheme built around moody colours works as well in a natural modern city apartment as in a retro modern home, and remember that these dark colours needn't be restricted to a light-filled property: they work just as well in a shady interior.

OPPOSITE Choose darker colours with a keen eye for the available natural light in a room. While sombre shades can work with naturally dark rooms, it's also fun to play with contrasts. Here, that is provided by the dramatic shards of sunlight against the chocolate brown of the walls.

RIGHT When opting for a deep shade, it can be as effective to use it on just one wall panel as to use it all over the room. In this chic dining room, one wall painted in fig green provides a great background for a white oak-veneer table.

It takes courage to use deep paint colours and/or dark surfaces on the floor, yet it creates drama and ambience. To lighten the effect, you could paint one of the walls in a paler organic paint. Or introduce dark tones via a strongly coloured naturally textured wall surface. Walls in clay plaster, for example, will appear moody and mid-toned, while one or two panelled walls using recycled wood with a rich, dark patina can look very dramatic. Dark fabrics feel enveloping and – when they are used for upholstery – are also extremely practical. But look out for fabrics with an unusual, rough, irregular weave or a self-pattern to create interest, and think of ways to add natural highlights. For example, you might pick trimmings in a lighter

ABOVE Adding warm-toned colour to a room can make it feel cosier, but using it on a ceiling creates a particularly cocooning effect. This room combines sunny yellow walls and a deeper toned ceiling with a pale floor and wood.

ABOVE RIGHT One strong splash of accent colour can heighten the irregular textures of natural surfaces. In this country kitchen, the teal blue of the back door highlights the variegated shades of the terracotta floor tiles.

shade, for instance adding a natural jute fringe to a black wool curtain or some opalescent shell buttons to a dark hessian cushion.

In a dark-toned room, the detailing and finishes of the furniture and accessories need careful thought, too. For a dramatically dark yet natural look, team textured walls with wood furniture featuring an obvious grain, use tactile fabrics and have natural-fibre rugs on the floor. But for a more decorative, glamorous finish, pick furniture with a glossy surface – highly polished timber, for example, or a sophisticated marble-topped table – and include plenty of mirrors and perhaps even an antique crystal chandelier.

BRIGHT COLOUR

In an ideal world, the healthiest and most unaffected interior will rely wholly on natural, unpainted surfaces and unbleached, undyed fabrics. But with judicious research, it's perfectly possible to find eco-sound products that introduce vibrant shades, so you can enjoy colour without worrying about the dire effects that dyes and pigments are having on the wider world.

Introducing colour to walls or floors using eco-sound paint is the easiest way to bring brilliance into the natural home. Don't overpower a room by painting all the walls in a bright shade: instead, paint just one feature wall. A painted floor in a strong colour is best in a bathroom or kitchen, or add brilliance along the edge with a painted border. And check that the colour will sit well with the natural surfaces you're including. For example, blue-toned paint, from lilac to rose, will look better teamed with cooler toned stone colours, such as greys, black and off-whites, whereas richer, yellow-toned colours like burnt orange or leaf green blend well with honey-toned wood, bamboo or cork. Also check that bold paint and upholstery colours won't overpower the delicacy of any natural tones and patterns in the room.

For those who prefer a classic 'natural' scheme but want a splash of colour, then a hand-painted recycled card lampshade, modern art on the walls, or a vibrant, vegetable-dyed rug could be the answer. In a bedroom, you might choose to add fairtrade bedlinen in zingy shades of amethyst or lime or a beautiful, colourful hand-embroidered, hemp bedcover.

ABOVE True, strong colour is best used in a contemporary interior. Sections of wall in jewel shades, combined with sleek natural textures, add a modern, architectural mood and help to define different areas in an open-plan interior.

ABOVE LEFT Paint isn't the only option for introducing colour. Look for materials with natural textures, from stone to wood, that come in unusual shades. Here blue Indian slate tiles and colourful mosaics create a pleasing mix.

THIS PAGE The unique textures and contours of items made from natural materials, from wicker baskets to jute string and from carved wood bowls to hand-thrown pottery, offer the opportunity for some satisfying finishing touches in the natural home.

Natural Details

In our hearts we all know that it is the little details that make the difference to a home. It is the carefully selected trimmings and decorative accessories, the ornaments and the art, that add personality, originality and a touch of soul. Including finishing touches with a 'natural' slant might also make you reflect on other ways to follow a natural, eco-sound way of life. That may mean switching to organic bath and beauty treats, using green cleaning products or scenting the home with vegetable-wax candles and essential oils.

The best news is that, with the growth of fairtrade merchandise and environmentally friendly products, and the commitment by many retailers to stocking organic home items, there has been a meteoric rise in interest in the design of desirable products made from recycled elements, and the choice of ethical yet beautiful accessories is set to grow still more. As well as organic ranges in the high-street stores, there are increasingly sophisticated eco websites with chic interior products on offer, and many young designers will only create work that follows firm ethical principles. There has also been a rise in the number of 'green' fairs, where you can source original, beautifully crafted goods. But don't forget that your own recycled or 'found' objects, from that nineteenth-century glass medicine bottle spied on the river bank to the giant pebble that you use as a doorstop, will bring the greatest pleasure of all.

OPPOSITE TOP LEFT Invest in a piece made by a contemporary craftsperson. Here, a bowl by Rupert Spira is artfully displayed to show off its shape and texture.

OPPOSITE TOP RIGHT Watch out for old wooden chairs that you can restore to life with a coat of paint and a comfortable cushion.

OPPOSITE CENTRE LEFT A simple setting focuses all the attention on the beautiful craftsmanship of a dramatic ethnic piece.

OPPOSITE CENTRE RIGHT Combine one-off items of furniture fashioned from recycled timber or driftwood with modern pieces for a particularly striking look.

OPPOSITE BELOW LEFT For the natural-texture magpie, the most utilitarian items can become objects of beauty. Here, rope and twine look very apealing when displayed en masse.

OPPOSITE BELOW RIGHT Found objects like shells, pebbles, cones and leaves have a special place in the natural home. Choosing the prettiest examples is half the fun.

HANDMADE

THIS PAGE Buying a one-off piece, whether a delicate ceramic bowl or a vase fashioned from recycled paper, can be immensely satisfying. Choose things that please you, rather than for their investment potential.

OPPPOSITE Amassing a collection of a certain genre of objects, from antique baskets to ethnic masks or straw hats, can prompt new ideas for display. Either line them up symmetrically or hang them casually from a wall or ceiling.

Not all handmade objects are created using natural materials – but most of them are. In today's world of identikit, mass-produced goods, it can be very gratifying to buy handmade one-offs, not least because you end up with something unique. If a decorative item features a slightly wobbly contour or an almost imperceptible irregularity, so much the better: this is what adds character. When looking for handmade pieces, think about cost, quality and originality. Items made abroad, in a developing country, may be remarkably good value, as well as being beautifully made and charmingly unique. By contrast, a handcrafted piece by a home-grown artist that uses natural or recycled materials may be just as beautiful, but will command a higher price, precisely because it is by a named artist and is being sold as 'art'.

LOCAL CRAFTS

The major benefit of buying close to home is that, as well as supporting local eco-minded or artists' communities, you will avoid the carbon footprint that is produced by transportation. It also offers the chance to commission a special piece by a particular craftsperson, or visit their studio to see the work in progress. Local crafts can include anything from hand-loomed textiles to earthenware pottery, wood carving to embroidery. Increasingly, there are

LEFT Pick out unique bowls, plates or vases to add character at home. Increasingly, shops are commissioning fairtrade suppliers to create modern designs using traditional techniques.

OPPOSITE When devising a display of handmade objects, try to keep it flexible so that new finds can be added later on. This display of handmade rustic shovels can easily accommodate more.

artists and craftspeople who produce organic goods, for example, making organic woollen rugs from wool produced by small farms or furniture from sustainable timber. Make it your business to find out what is going on locally by visiting craft fairs and local galleries.

FAIRTRADE SUPPLIERS

In recent years, there has been plenty of publicity about fairtrade merchandise and we would all do well to support this valuable initiative. Fairtrade seeks to provide greater equity in international trade for small producers and makers, often – though not always – in developing countries. The fairtrade set-up offers family businesses and small co-operatives better trading and working conditions, a fairer wage, and the chance for women to achieve more equality through work. It also helps to preserve traditional crafts around the world.

A quick glance at any range of fairtrade interiors merchandise shows a wide variety of choices. For instance, you will find glorious hand-loomed and embroidered textiles for cushion covers and throws, carved wooden bowls and platters, sometimes hand-decorated with mother-of-pearl from recycled shells, and handmade paper lampshades incorporating delicate leaves and flowers. Those who prefer a modern interior may feel put off buying fairtrade goods because most have an ethnic look. Increasingly, however, there are Western companies that are committed to creating design-conscious goods with a modern appeal, but produced by fairtrade co-operatives. By buying these products, it's possible to get the best of both worlds. There are also websites specialising in luxury fairtrade merchandise, offering items such as embroidered silk bed throws and hand-loomed cashmere throws.

PERSONAL

It's easy to assume that we need to buy all our home accessories from shops or websites, yet spare a thought for the beautiful, handmade pieces that we can create ourselves. Many of us aren't naturally inclined to handicrafts, but we can gain great satisfaction from rediscovering the traditional skills with which our grandparents used to create essential home items. It can be relaxing (and even fun) to knit a cushion cover using giant needles and a skein of organic wool, to crochet a blanket using wool you have unravelled from a cast-off jumper, or to hand-trim with vintage ribbon a patchwork cushion made from a pair of old curtains.

FOUND

Who hasn't picked up a handful of pretty shells or an attractive piece of bark from the forest floor? Children, in particular, have the knack of collecting everything from stones to conkers and slivers of driftwood. While none of us should be actively pillaging the natural world, there's nothing wrong with collecting beautiful 'found' objects and displaying them artfully at home. It's the ultimate way to bring nature's beauty into our lives.

NATURAL FINDS
It's worth considering why we pick up finds in the first place. Is it because we want to hold them, enjoy their texture, examine their intricate patterns and marvel at their subtlety of colour? For those of us who are urban-dwellers, is it because we are starved of natural substances and surrounded by too many man-made materials? Or is it that, by bringing a tiny piece of nature back from a certain place, we hope it will capture a particular memory? Either way,

BELOW LEFT Choosing the right container to show off pebbles, shells or seed pods, is as important as the natural objects themselves. A bright bowl provides a good contrast.

BELOW Tailor your display of natural objects according to the interior style at home. This tableau looks elegant because the fragile animal skull has been arranged in a sophisticated glass vase.

OPPOSITE Keep an eye open for vintage natural finds. The fragility of these antique shells adds extra interest: butterfly collections, old ostrich eggs and vintage feathers also make very appealing displays.

make sure you gather treasures that mean something to you and try to pick items that won't deteriorate. Stones and shells should be washed in clean water and carefully dried, leaves should be pressed. Bark or driftwood can be gently dried in the airing cupboard.

FOUND OBJECTS

Trawls through the countryside will sometimes highlight 'found' but not necessarily natural objects. River banks and the seashore are particularly good hunting grounds for items that have been washed up, from green glass apothecary bottles to coins or ceramic pots. Those travelling further afield might be able to pick up old, ethnic 'found' items that – in a developing country – are no longer quite so prized, from carved wooden bowls to simple agricultural tools. Either way, it seems a crime to throw away these simple treasures. Quite often, their journey through the waste stream or through sea or river will have created gently eroded contours or an unusual patina. Enjoy the fleeting questions behind each item's origin – who owned it, how far has it travelled?

USING FOUND OBJECTS

The simplest way to get pleasure from found objects is to display them to show off their textural and visual appeal (see pages 76–77). Yet it can also be deeply satisfying to incorporate them into a decorative scheme, on however grand or small a scale. Attractive pebbles, for example, can be drilled with a small hole (a glazier should be able to do this for you), then threaded onto a light pull. Larger shells may be stuck onto plain curtain finials using strong glue. Think laterally, too. Trace the silhouette of a giant leaf, for example, then transfer the shape onto a plain organic cotton cushion cover, and backstitch the outline in a contrast thread.

BECOME A MAGPIE. CULTIVATE THE ART OF EXAMINING AND COLLECTING. ENJOYING A COLLECTION OF SPECIAL FOUND OBJECTS AT HOME SHOULD BECOME THE HABIT OF A LIFETIME

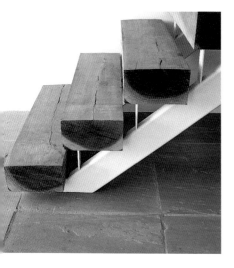

RECYCLED

Recycling isn't just about using reclaimed building materials, surfaces, fittings and furniture. It's also possible to create inventive home accessories using smaller recycled items and textiles. Get into the habit of examining everything before you throw it out. Can you make something useful or decorative out of it, or can you give it to someone else who can?

DESIGNER RECYCLED PIECES

There is a vast amount of imaginative new design work coming from eco-minded designers who are committed to 'repurposing' wasted fabrics, paper

ABOVE Successful recycling is all about adopting a new, creative mindset. Old railway sleepers or hunks of timber from a tree blown down in a storm and resawn, can be 'repurposed' as fabulous staircase treads.

RIGHT The satisfying aspect of recycling small, domestic items is that - precisely because each one has survived over time - they continue to give good service. Here, old chopping boards are practical and enduring.

OPPOSITE A trip to a country jumble sale or junk shop can result in a fascinating selection of objects to recycle. Here, a clever combination of everything from an old egg basket used to store soap to a modern perfume bottle, sets an elegant tone.

Recycling doesn't only mean buying things that other people have made. It's just as possible to create quirky accessories yourself using inexpensive bargains picked up in a junk shop or inherited from a relative. An old picture frame, gently distressed but still solid, can be reused with a fresh mount or an eccentric 1950s silk lampshade may be salvaged, trimmed with tiny vintage buttons and teamed with a new lamp base. Equally, a junk-shop chair can be given a new lease of life by re-upholstering in a patchwork of vintage fabrics or a shabby table can be painted in a fresh, funky colour. The eclectic vintage look is becoming a decorative style in its own right, so don't be afraid to embrace it. Have a swap party with friends as someone else's junk might mean a great new accessory for you.

RECYCLED MATERIALS

There are also many highly imaginative products available to buy that have been deliberately made from new materials created from recycled objects. These might be witty little items, such as a soap dish or computer mouse mat made from reconstituted rubber tyres, or a wool throw rewoven from wool fibres salvaged from old jumpers. Alternatively, you might manage to find a home for a pretty card lampshade made from 100 per cent recycled cardboard or for a decorative glass tabletop panel that has been created using recycled glass. There are also artists who use recycling to create new artworks, whether making old pulped books into pots or turning discarded plates into ornamental one-offs using paint and collage. Eco-conscious designers and suppliers are often only too happy to detail the 'green' origins of their new pieces. And isn't it much more satisfying to know the story behind a special new home accessory?

and detritus, and turning them into quirky, thoughtful new items for the home. Our landfill sites are full of cast-off textiles, so it is a relief to see enterprising designers using everything from old train-seat fabrics and second-hand vintage men's ties to swatches collected from textile sample books, and turning them into designer cushions, peg bags, lavender sachets or even Christmas decorations. For a rustic look, there are specialist companies that create cushion covers using vintage grain sacks, or that cut up antique linen sheets and make them into tablelinen. Once you've seen the inventive nature of these products, it seems a crime to buy new! Search the internet for websites that specialise in these eco-designs, or visit the art-school degree shows to snap up new talent. Many designers will also be happy to create a bespoke design, perhaps embroidered with your initials or a special date.

THIS PAGE Match recycled objects to the architecture at home. In this period interior, it was appropriate to use gently distressed objects to highlight the beauty of the old beams and plasterwork.

OPPOSITE Making a commitment to scour reclamation yards for unusual small fittings, from taps to door handles, will result in a creative interior. Here, a stone sink, timber stand and reclaimed taps have resulted in a rustic yet decorative bathroom.

Suppliers

AUSTRALIA

BIOME
215 Adelaide Street
Brisbane City
Tel: +61 (0) 7 3368 3009
biome.com.au
Sustainable, organic products
such as bamboo teasets,
organic bed linen and hemp-
flax towels.

ECO DEPOT
Tel: +61 (0) 2 4283 8232
ecodepot.com.au
Wide selection of eco gadgets
and recycled homewares.

GECOZ
85a Hyde Street
Bellingen NSW 2454
Tel: +61 (0) 2 6655 0755
gecoz.net.au
Everything from bio paints
and organic bedding to
recycled bedspreads.

EUROPE

DURO SWEDEN
Box 907
5-801 32 Gavle, Sweden
Tel: +46 26 65 65 00
durosweden.se
Environmentally friendly
wallpapers in many designs.

ECONHOME
econhome.net
The website for the initiative
to reduce energy consumption
across Europe.

LA MAISON DE LA
FAUSSE FOURRURE
Tel: + 33 1 49 62 1087
lamaisondelafaussefourrure.com
French-based company
offering beautiful cushions,
throws and hot water bottle
covers in fake fur.

SAHCO HESSLEIN
GmbH & Co KG
Kreuzburger Str 17-19
D-90 471 Nuremberg, Germany

Tel: +49 (0) 911 99 87-0
sahcohesslein.com
Wide selection of fabrics
including silks and linen.

VORWERK & CO
Teppichwerke GmbH
Kulmannstrasse 11
31785 Hamein, Germany
Tel: + 49 (0) 5151 103 734
vorwerk-carpet.com
100% wool carpets.

5 QM
Gladbacher Str 35
D-50672 K In
Cologne, Germany
Tel: +49 (0) 221 2948456
5qm.de
Store selling original vintage
50s, 60s and 70s wallpapers.

USA

AMERICAN SALVAGE
Tel: +1-305-691-7001
Salvage, from recycled
furniture to architectural
fittings.

BAMBOO HARDWOODS
4100 4th Avenue South
Seattle, WA 98134
Tel: +1-206-264-2414
bamboohardwoods.com
Wide selection of bamboo
flooring and furniture.

CHABA DÉCOR
12300 E Washington
Boulevard, Suite K
Whittier, CA 90606
Tel: +1-562-320-0298
chabadecor.com
Furniture and artworks made
using recycled wood from
Thailand.

DIRT CANDLES
1880 West 10th Street, Unit 106
Riviera Beach FL 33404-6436
Tel: +1-866-436-3865
dirtcandles.com
Organically grown US soybean
candles with fresh flowers and
herbs.

FRIENDS OF WATER
1307 NE 146th Avenue
Vancouver WA 98684
Tel: +1-866-482-6803
friendsofwater.com
Offers help and advice on
saving water.

GREEN BUILDING
RESOURCES GUIDE
greenguide.com
Database of green building
materials and products.

GREEN HOME
PO Box 42676
Washington DC 20015
Tel: +1-202-544-5336
greenhome.org
Promotion of affordable
sustainable design and
awareness of green practices.

HOME ENERGY SAVER
hes.lbl.gov
Online DIY home energy audit.

MOD GREEN POD
Tel: +1-617-670-2000
modgreenpod.com
Beautiful organic wallpapers
and fabrics.

O ECO TEXTILES
942 18th Avenue East
Seattle, Washington 98112
Tel: +1-206-633-1177
oecotextiles.com
Luxurious, beautiful range of
eco furnishing fabrics.

THE OLD-FASHIONED MILK
PAINT COMPANY
436 Main Street
Groton
Maine 01450
Tel: +1-978-448-6336
milkpaint.com
Organic milk paints specialists.

ROOFSCAPES
7114 McCallum Street
Philadelphia
Pennsylvania PA 19119-2935
Tel: +1-215-247-8784
roofmeadow.com

Information and links for
green roof design.

SOLAR ENERGY INDUSTRIES
ASSOCATION
805 15th Street, NW 510
Washington DC 20005
Tel: +1-202-682-0556
seia.org
National trade association of
companies providing solar
products

TOMORROW'S WORLD
9647 First View Street,
Norfolk
VA 23503
Tel: +1-800-229-7571
tomorrowsworld.com
Organic mattresses, towels
and natural candles.

USA GREEN BUILDING
COUNCIL
1800 Massachusetts Avenue N W
Suite 300
Washington DC 20036
Tel: +1-800-795-1747
usgbc.org
Online courses; information
about green building.

UK

Green Energy Information
BIG GREEN SWITCH
biggreenswitch.co.uk
An easy online guide to
creating a greener lifestyle.

BRITISH WOOL MARKETING
BOARD
Wool House
Roydsdale Way
Euroway Trading Estate
Bradford
West Yorkshire BD4 6SE
Tel: +44 (0) 1274 688666
britishwool.org.uk
Information about British wool
including information about
wool insulation and bedding.

ENERGY SAVING TRUST
energysavingtrust.org.uk
Tel: +44 (0)800 512 012

Impartial advice on CO$_2$ emissions and climate change.

ENVIRONMENT AGENCY
PO Box 544
Rotherham S60 1BY
environment-agency.gov.uk
Protection of the environment in England and Wales; website offers information on air quality, conservation and water.

FRIENDS OF THE EARTH
26-28 Underwood Street
London N1 7JQ
Tel: +44 (0) 20 7490 1555
foe.co.uk
Information website, plus online green shop.

LOW IMPACT LIVING INITIATIVE
Redfield Community
Winslow
Bucks MK18 3LZ
Tel: +44 (0) 1296 714184
lowimpact.org
Non-profit organisation with information on eco building, plus courses.

THE NATIONAL ENERGY FOUNDATION
Davy Avenue
Knowlhill
Milton Keynes MK5 8NG
Tel: +44 (0) 1908 665555
nef.org.uk
Committed to energy saving and developing small-scale UK renewable energy sources.

WATERWISE
1 Queen Anne's Gate
London SW1H 9BT
Tel: +44 (0) 20 7957 4615
waterwise.org.uk
NGO committed to reducing water consumption; website with tips on saving water.

Heating
AGA
Station Road
Ketley
Telford
Shropshire TF1 5AQ
Tel: +44 (0) 1952 642000
aga-web.co.uk

Full range of cast-iron stoves and appliances.

BRITISH GAS
britishgas.co.uk
Advice on energy-efficient products and how to get a home energy check.

Bathrooms
AQUALISA
Aqualisa Products
The Flyer's Way
Westerham
Kent TN16 1DE
Tel: +44 (0) 1959 560000
aqualisa.co.uk
Shower specialists.

CP HART
Newnham Terrace
Hercules Road
London SE1 7DR
Tel: +44 (0) 20 7902 1000
cphart.co.uk
Modern and traditional bathroom fittings, baths and basins from natural materials.

Lighting
ENERGY BULBS
Tel: +44 (0) 1507 310124
energybulbs.co.uk
Online source of low-energy light bulbs plus information.

JOHN CULLEN LIGHTING
585 Kings Road
London SW6 2EH
Tel: +44 (0) 20 7371 5400
johncullenlighting.co.uk
Designer lighting with energy-saving light fittings.

Renewable Energy Sources
B & Q
diy.com
The DIY store has a green energy section selling solar panels and wind turbines.

GROUND-SOURCE HEAT PUMP ASSOCATION
(contact details as The National Energy Foundation)
gshp.org.uk
Information on ground-source heat pumps.

SOLAR TRADE ASSOCIATION
Tel: +44 (0) 1908 442290
solartradeassociation.org.uk
Information on solar power, plus list of installers.

Green Roofs
GREEN ROOFS
greenroofs.co.uk
Information website on all aspects of green roofs.

LIVING ROOFS
livingroofs.org
Independent UK website dedicated to research, advance and promotion of green roofs.

Natural Paints and Wood Products
AURO ORGANIC PAINTS
Cheltenham Road
Bisley, Stroud
Gloucestershire GL6 7BX
Tel: +44 (0) 1452 772020
auro.co.uk
Paints that use natural and organic raw materials, plus wood finishes and waxes.

ECOPAINTS
Braintree Enterprise Centre
46 Springwood Drive
Braintree CM7 2YN
Tel: +44 (0) 845 345 7725
natural-paints.co.uk
Good selection of natural paints.

IEKO
27A Hartfield Road
Forest Row
East Sussex RH18 5DY
Tel: +44 (0) 1342 824466
ieko.co.uk
Full range of natural paints and wood products.

NATURAL DECO
The Technocentre
Puma Way
Coventry CV1 2TT
Tel: +44 (0) 2476 792607
naturaldeco.co.uk
Wonderful online store offering natural paints, natural building materials and woodcare.

NUTSHELL NATURAL PAINTS
Unit 3, Leigham Units
Silverton Road
Matford Park
Exeter, Devon EX2 8HY
Tel: +44 (0) 1392 823760
nutshellpaints.com
Wide variety of own-brand natural paints, wood finishes, waxes and varnishes.

Recycled Surfaces
DAPPLE GLASS
1 Brunswick House
Balcombe Street
London NW1 6NG
Tel: +44 (0) 20 7193 6211
dappleglass.com
Contemporary decorative architectural glass and glass tiles using recycled and eco-friendly materials.

Reclamation and Salvage
LASSCO
30 Wandsworth Road
Vauxhall
London SW8 2LG
Tel: +44 (0) 20 7394 2100
lassco.co.uk
Architectural antiques, salvage items and curiosities.

RETROUVIUS
2A Ravensworth Road
Kensal Green
London NW10 5NR
Tel: +44 (0) 20 8960 6060
retrouvius.co.uk
Wide range of architectural salvage items including a useful design service.

Stone
FIRED EARTH
3 Twyford Mill
Oxford Road
Adderbury, Near Banbury
Oxfordshire OX17 3SX
Tel: +44 (0) 1295 812088
firedearth.com
Slate, stone and terracotta flooring, plus wood and natural-fibre flooring.

MANDARIN STONE
Unit 1, Wonastow Industrial Estate
Monmouth
Monmouthshire NP25 5JB

Tel: +44 (0) 1600 715444
mandarinstone.co.uk
Large choice of granite,
marble, travertine, basalt and
slate, supplied and installed.

STONE AGE
Unit 3, Parsons Green Depot
Parsons Green Lane
London SW6 4HH
Tel: +44 (0) 20 7384 9090
estone.co.uk
Travertine, limestone,
sandstone, marble and more.

STONELL
521-525 Battersea Park Road
London SW11 3BN
Tel: +44 (0) 800 083 2283
stonell.com
Natural stone including
limestone, slate, riven slate
and hand-aged stone tiles.

Sustainable Furniture
IT'S RECLAIMED
Tel: +44 (0) 20 8245 6679
itsreclaimed.co.uk
Mainly commissioned
furniture, picture and mirror
frames using reclaimed wood.

PLI DESIGN
Unit 15, 62 Tritton Road
London SE21 8DE
Tel: +44 (0) 20 8670 6857
plidesign.co.uk
Designers and makers of
sustainable furniture.

Natural Building Materials
CONSTRUCTION RESOURCES
111 Rotherhithe Street
London SE16 4NF
Tel: +44 (0) 20 7232 1181
contructionresources.com
Ecological builder's
merchants, with everything
from natural insulation to
solar panels and rainwater-
harvesting equipment.

GREEN BUILDING STORE
Heath House Mill
Heath House Lane
Bolster Moor
West Yorkshire HD7 4JW
greenbuildingstore.co.uk
Online and mail-order: green
building materials for

sustainable and energy-
efficient homes.

GREENSPEC
greenspec.co.uk
Extremely informative
construction guide to green
building design and materials.

VC RESTORATIONS
VC Restoration
Moone Hall
Church Road
Stambourne
Halstead
Essex CO9 4NR
Tel: +44 (0) 1440 785054
vcrestorations.co.uk
Lime building materials.

Wood
SELECT VENEERS
Unit 3, The iO Centre
Whittle Way
Arlington Business Park
Gunnels Wood Road
Stevenage
Hertfordshire SG1 2BD
Tel: +44 (0) 1483 750880
selectveneers.com
Natural wood veneers.

THE ANTIQUE OAK FLOORING
COMPANY
94 High Street
London N8 7NT
Tel: +44 (0) 20 8347 8222
antiqueoakflooring.com
Reclaimed timber and flooring;
new solid wood floors.

Lino, Bamboo and Cork Flooring
THE BAMBOO FLOORING
COMPANY
114 Kitchener Road
Leicester LE5 4AT
Tel: +44 (0) 116 274 1050
bambooflooringcompany.com
Specialists in bamboo flooring
and accessories.

SIMPLY BAMBOO
18 Fernwood Rise
Brighton
East Sussex BN1 5EP
Tel: +44 (0) 845 222 0408
simplybamboo.co.uk
Bamboo flooring in a choice of
colours and finishes.

SINCLAIR TILL
793 Wandsworth Bridge Road
London SW8 3JQ
Tel: +44 (0) 20 7720 0031
sinclairtill.co.uk
Wood, lino and natural
flooring; expert fitting advice.

Leather
ALMA HOME
12-14 Greatorex Street
London E1 5NF
Tel: +44 (0) 20 7377 0762
almahome.co.uk
Every type of leather and
animal skin, bespoke or off-
the-peg; accessories including
cushions, beanbags and rugs.

BENSON DESIGN
Tel: +44 (0) 20 8452 8864
bensondesign.com
Bespoke leather flooring and
rugs.

BILL AMBERG
21-22 Chepstow Corner
London W2 4XE
Tel: +44 (0) 20 7727 3560
billamberg.com
Bespoke leather interiors,
including floors and walls;
leather storage and
accessories.

Wool Carpet
BRINTONS CARPETS
PO Box 16
Exchange Street
Kidderminster
Worcestershire DY10 1AG
Tel: +44 (0) 800 505055
brintons.net
Fine quality wool carpets with
a wide choice of styles,
colours and weaves.

FLEETWOOD FOX
96 Springfield Road
Wellington
Somerset TA21 8LH
Tel: +44 (0) 1823 667337
fleetwoodfox.com
Flatweave carpets woven to
order using British and New
Zealand wool.

ROGER OATES DESIGN
1 Munro Terrace
Cheyne Walk

London SW10 0DL
Tel: +44 (0) 20 7351 2288
rogeroates.com
100% wool flatweave and
Wilton narrow-width carpets in
herringbones and stripes.

Natural-Fibre Flooring
CRUCIAL TRADING
The Plaza
535 Kings Road
London SW10 0SZ
Tel: +44 (0) 20 7376 7100
crucial-trading.com
Many types of natural flooring
including seagrass, coir, jute,
paper and bamboo.

THE ALTERNATIVE FLOORING
COMPANY
3B Stephenson Close
East Portway
Andover
Hampshire SP10 3RU
Tel: +44 (0) 1264 335111
alternativeflooring.com
Big range of natural-fibre
flooring, including coir, sisal,
jute, seagrass and wool mixes.

Fabrics
ANTA
Fearn
Tain
Ross-shire IV20 1XW
Tel: +44 (0) 1862 832477
anta.co.uk
Pure wool and linen fabrics on
the roll, including tartan, plus
carpets, throws and furniture.

HARLANDS ORGANIC
FURNISHINGS
Cat Hill Gallery
264 Merton Road
Southfields
London SW18 5JL
Tel: +44 (0) 7984 635726
organic-furnishings.co.uk
Organic fabrics, including
100% organic printed cotton
and cotton-hemp; wool textiles.

IAN MANKIN
109 Regents Park Road
London NW1 8UR
Tel: +44 (0) 20 7722 0997
ianmankin.co.uk
Classic utility fabrics, including
ticking, calico, and cottons.

JOHN BOYD TEXTILES
Higher Flax Mills
Castle Cary
Somerset
BA7 7DY
Tel: +44 (0) 1963 350451
johnboydtextiles.co.uk
Specialist weavers and
suppliers of fine horsehair
fabrics.

LINEN FABRICS
linenfabrics.co.uk
Mail-order heavy and medium-
weight linens, plus sheers and
embroidered fabrics.

MALABAR
31-33 The South Bank
Business Centre
Ponton Road
London SW8 5BL
Tel: +44 (0) 20 7501 4200
malabar.co.uk
Wide choice of Indian yard-
dyed and hand-loomed
interior textiles including
stripes, plain, sheers and
embroidered fabrics.

PARNA
parna.co.uk
Website offering hand-crafted
vintage textiles, including
embroidered wall hangings,
linen and hemp cushion
covers and table runners.

RUSSELL AND CHAPPLE
68 Drury Lane
London WC2B 5SP
Tel: +44 (0) 20 7497 7521
russellandchapple.co.uk
Theatrical suppliers; canvas
and natural furnishing fabrics.

VOLGA LINEN COMPANY
17 Langton Street
London SW10 0JL
Tel: +44 (0) 1728 633091
volgalinen.co.uk
100% linen fabrics on the roll,
plus tablelinen and bedlinen.

WHALEYS (BRADFORD) LTD
Harris Court
Great Horton
Bradford
West Yorkshire BD7 4EQ
Tel: +44 (0) 1274 576718

whaleys-bradford.ltd.uk
Stockists of many types of
calico, butter muslin, jute,
cotton, linen and silk.

Wallpapers
GRAHAM & BROWN
Tel: +44 (0) 800 328 8452 for
stockists
grahamandbrown.co.uk
Wallpapers in many styles,
printed on either recycled
paper or paper from managed
forests, using non-acidic inks.

Organic/Eco Home
Accessories
DRAPERS ORGANIC
PO Box 588
Godstone RH9 8WX
Tel: +44 (0) 8452 603560
drapersorganiccotton.co.uk
100% organic cotton and
hemp products including
tableware, cushion covers and
curtains.

GREENFIBRES
99 High Street
Totnes
Devon TQ9 5PF
Tel: +44 (0) 1803 868001
greenfibres,com
Online site devoted to organic
bedding, mattress pads, wool,
towels and clothing.

LAZY ENVIRONMENTALIST
lazye.co.uk
Beautiful, indulgent website
with organic cotton bath
sheets, all-natural candles and
hand-stitched quilts using
vintage fabrics.

NIGEL'S ECO STORE
55 Coleridge Street
Hove BN3 5AB
Tel: +44 (0) 800 288 8970
nigelsecostore.com
Vast array of eco lifestyle
products, plus energy-saving
devices.

THE NATURAL STORE
Tel: +44 (0)1273 746781
thenaturalstore.col.uk
Online boutique featuring
stylish and luxurious organic,
vintage, fairtrade and eco

home products, plus beauty,
food and gifts.

Fairtrade
LUMA DIRECT
PO Box 28894
London SW13 0WH
Tel: +44 (0) 845 094 2598
lumadirect.com
Organic bedding, linen and silk
throws and cashmere throws
produced by fairtrade
cooperatives.

THE BOMBAY BEDSPREAD
COMPANY
14 Pelham Court
Kingston Road
Staines
Middlesex TW18 1AL
Tel: +44 (0) 1784 465574
bombaybedspread.com
Fairtrade retailer of Indian
bedspreads, cushion covers
and quilts.

TRAIDCRAFT SHOP
Traidcraft plc
Kingsway
Gateshead
Tyne and Wear NE11 0NE
Tel: +44 (0) 845 330 8901
traidcraftshop.co.uk
Wide choice of fairtrade home,
food and fashion products.

Decorative Natural
Accessories/Furniture
BEYOND THE SEA
22 Middle Street
Padstow
Cornwall PL28 8AB
Tel: +44 (0) 1841 533588
beyondthesea.co.uk
Handmade driftwood furniture
made to order.

EMILY READETT BAYLEY
Elmtree House Gallery
54 Main Road
Long Bennington
Newark
Nottinghamshire NG23 5DJ
Tel: +44 (0) 1400 281563
emilyreadettbayley.com
Decorative accessories,
including hand-sewn cockerel
feather fans, mother-of-pearl
cutlery, driftwood picture
frames.

PAPILIO
Bethany
5 Allington Road
Newick
Lewes
East Sussex BN8 4NA
Tel: +44 (0) 1825 723434
papilio.co.uk
Natural shell cabinet handles,
mother-of-pearl place
settings, feather and leather
trims and natural shell and
pebble curtain trimmings.

THE FEATHER FACTORY
Upper Wake Cottage
Kingstone
Ilminster
Somerset TA19 0NT
Tel: +44 (0) 1460 55410
thefeatherfactory.co.uk
Many types of natural
feathers, including peacock,
pheasant, goose and ostrich.

Designer Recycled
Accessories
ARMADILLO DESIGNS
12 Allard Gardens
Briarwood Road
London SW4 9QA
Tel: +44 (0) 20 7720 0695
finefayre.co.uk/armadillodesigns
Decorative accessories;
cushions and pouffes made
from vintage jeans.

CREATIVELY RECYCLED
EMPIRE
creativelyrecycledempire.co.uk
Cushions made from recycled
London underground train
seats.

REVAMPIT
52 Grafton Road
London W3 6PD
Tel: +44 (0) 20 8354 7354
revampit.co.uk
Textile accessories such as
cushion covers and lavender
bags in vintage fabrics.

USE IT
Tel: +44 (0) 7887 521102
use-uk.com
Eco-friendly accessories;
lampshades made from 100%
recycled cardboard and
cushions from sample books.

Architects & Designers

1100 ARCHITECT
435 Hudson Street
New York NY 10014
USA
Tel: +1 (212) 645 1011
1100architect.com

ABRAHAM & THAKORE LTD
D351 Defence Colony
New Delhi 110024
India
Tel: + 91 11 699 3714

ALBERTO PINTO
Hotel de Victoire
11 rue d'Aboukir
75002 Paris
France
Tel: + 33 (0) 1 4013 0000
albertopinto.com

ALEX VAN DE WALLE
Vlaamsesteenweg 3
1000 Brussels
Belgium
Tel: + 32 (0) 477 806 676
alex.vdw@swing.be

ANDERSON MASON DALE ARCHITECTS
1615 Seventeenth Street
Denver Colorado 80202
USA
Tel: +1 (303) 294 9448
amdarchitects.com

ARCHITECTUS
1 Centre Street
P O Box 90621
AMSC
Freemans Bay
Auckland
New Zealand
Tel: +64 (0) 9 307 5970
architectus.com.au

AXEL VERVOORDT
Kasteel van's-Gravenwezel
Sint Jobsteenweg 64
2970's-Gravenwezel
Belgium
Tel: + 32 (0) 3 680 1489
axel-vervoordt.com

BERNIE DE LA CUONA
Mistress Page's House
13a High Street
Windsor
Berks SL4 1LD
England
Tel: +44 (0) 1753 830301

BILHUBER & ASSOCIATES
330 East 59th Street
New York NY 10022
USA
Tel: + 1 (212) 308 4888
bilhuber.com

BKK ARCHITECTS
Level 9
180 Russell Street
Melbourne 3000
Victoria
Australia
Tel: + 61 (0) 3 9671 4555
b-k-k.com.au

CATHERINE MEMMI
11 rue Saint Sulpice
75006 Paris
France
Tel: + 33 (0) 1 44 07 22 28
Tel: + 1 (212) 226 8200
catherinememmi.com

CLINTON MURRAY ARCHITECTS
2 King Street
Merimbula
New South Wales 2548
Australia
Tel: + 61 (0) 2 6495 1964
clintonmurray.com.au

COLLECTION PRIVÉE
Gilles Pellerin
9 rue des États-Unis
06400 Cannes
France
Tel: + 33 (0) 4 97 06 94 94
collection-privee.com

COLLETT-ZARZYCKI
Fernhead Studios
2b Fernhead Road
London W9 3ET
England
Tel: + 44 (0) 20 8969 6967
collett-zarzycki.com

DANIEL ROMUALDEZ ARCHITECTS
119 West 23rd Street
New York NY 10011
USA
Tel: + 1 (212) 989 8429

DOMINIQUE KIEFFER
8 rue Hérold
75001 Paris
France
Tel: + 33 (0) 1 42 21 32 44
dkieffer.com

ÉRIC GIZARD ASSOCIÉS
14 rue Crespin du Cast
75011 Paris
France
Tel: + 33 (0) 1 55 28 38 58
gizardassocies.com

FORMA DESIGNS
Luigi Esposito
160 Walton Street
London SW3 2JL
England
Tel: + 44 (0) 20 7581 2500
formadesigns.co.uk

FRANK FAULKNER
92 North 5th Street
Hudson
New York NY 12534
USA
Tel: + 1 (518) 828 2295

FRÉDÉRIC MÉCHICHE
14 rue Saint Croix de la Bretonne
Paris 75004
France
Tel: +33 (0) 1 4278 7828

GENE LEEDY ARCHITECT
55 Ave G NW
Winter Haven
Florida 33880
USA
Tel: + 1 (863) 293 7173
geneleedyarchitect.com

HEIBERG CUMMINGS DESIGN
9 West 19th Street
3rd Floor
New York NY 10011
USA
Tel: + 1 (212) 337 2030
hcd3.com

HENNIE INTERIORS AS
Helene Forbes-Hennie
Thomles Gate 4
0270 Oslo
Norway
Tel: + 47 22 06 85 86

HUBERT ZANDBERG INTERIORS
Studio 106 Network Hub
300 Kensal Road
London W10 5BE
England
hzinteriors.com

HUDSON ARCHITECTS
49-59 Old Street
London EC1V 9HX
England
Tel: + 44 (0) 20 7490 3411
hudsonarchitects.co.uk

IPL INTERIORS
François Gilles
Studio 4a
75-81 Burnaby Street
London SW10 0NS
Tel: +44 (0) 20 7978 4224

JAMES GORST ARCHITECTS LTD
The House of Detention
Clerkenwell Close
London EC1R 0AS
England
Tel: +44 (0)20 7336 7140
jamesgorstarchitects.com

JOHN WARDLE ARCHITECTS
Level 10
180 Russell Street
Melbourne 3000
Victoria
Australia
Tel: + 61 3 9654 8700
johnwardle.com

JULIE PRISCA
46 rue du Bac
75007 Paris
France
Tel: + 33 (0) 1 45 48 13 29
julieprisca.com

KATHARINE POOLEY
160 Walton Street
London SW3 2JL
England
Tel: + 44 (0) 20 7584 3223
katharinepooley.com

KENYON KRAMER
Décoration Jardin
3 place des 3 Ormeaux
13100 Aix en Provence
France
Tel: + 33 (0) 4 42 23 52 32

LAUTNER ASSOCIATES
8055 W. Manchester Ave
Suite 705
Playa del Rey
California 90293
USA
Tel: +1 (310) 577 7783
lautnerassociates.com

LENA PROUDLOCK
4 The Chipping
Tetbury
Gloucestershire GL8 8ET
England
Tel: + 44 (0) 1666 500 051
lenaproudlock.com

LEONARDO CHALUPOWICZ
3527 Landa Street
Los Angeles
California 90039
USA
Tel: + 1 (323) 660 8261
chalupowicz.com

LINUM FRANCE SAS
Anna Bonde
ZAC du Tourail
Coustellet
84660 Maubec
France
Tel: + 33 (0) 4 90 76 34 00
linum-france.com

MARC PROSMAN
ARCHITECTEN BV
Overtoom 197
1054 HT Amsterdam
The Netherlands
Tel: +31 (0) 20 489 2099
prosman.nl

MOOARC
198 Blackstock Road
London N5 1EN, England
Tel: +44 (0) 20 7354 1729
mooarc.com

MURIEL BRANDOLINI
525 East 72nd Street
New York NY 10021
USA
Tel: + 1 (212) 249 4920
murielbrandolini.com

OGAWA/DEPARDON
ARCHITECTS
69 Mercer Street
2nd Floor
New York NY 10012
USA
Tel: +1 (212) 627 7390
oda-ny.com

PAOLO BADESCO
Viale di Porta Vercellina 5
20123 Milan
Italy
Tel: + 39 024 100737
paolobadesco.it

PERI WOLFMAN
periw@charlesgold.com

PIERRE D'AVOINE
ARCHITECTS
54-58 Tanner Street
London SE1 3PH
England
Tel: + 44 (0) 20 7403 7220
davoine.net

RAMÓN ESTEVE
Estudio de Arquitectura
Jorge Juan 8, 5°, 11a
46004 Valencia
Spain
Tel: + 34 96 351 0434
ramonesteve.com

REED DESIGN
151a Sydney Street
London SW3 6NT
England
Tel: + 44 (0) 20 7565 0066

SETH STEIN ARCHITECTS
15 Grand Union Centre
West Row
London W10 5AS
England
Tel: + 44 (0) 20 8968 8581
sethstein.com

SHARLAND & LEWIS
52 Long Street
Tetbury
Gloucestershire GL8 8AQ

England
Tel: + 44 (0) 1666 500354
sharlandandlewis.com

SHELTON, MINDEL &
ASSOCIATES
56 West 22ndStreet
12th Floor
New York NY 10010
USA
Tel: +1 (212) 206 6406
sheltonmindel.com

SLEE ARCHITECTS &
INTERIORS
101 Dorp Street
Stellenbosch 7600
South Africa
Tel: + 27 21 887 3385
slee.co.za

SOLIS BETANCOURT
1739 Connecticut Avenue NW
Washington
DC 20009
USA
Tel: + 1 (202) 659 8734
solisbetancourt.com

STEPHEN FALCKE INTERIOR
DESIGN CONSULTANTS
P O Box 1416
Parklands
Johannesburg 2121
South Africa
Tel: + 27 113 27 67 30

STEVEN EHRLICH
10865 Washington Boulevard
Culver City
California 90232
USA
Tel: + 1 (310) 838 9700
s-ehrlich.com

STICKLAND COOMBE
ARCHITECTS
258 Lavender Hill
London SW11 1LJ
England
Tel: + 44 (0) 20 7924 1699

STUDIO K O
Karl Fournier & Olivier Marty
7, Rue Geoffroy l'Angevin
75004 Paris
France
Tel: + 33 (0) 1 42 71 13 92
komarrakech@studioko.fr
koparis@studioko.fr

TERRY HUNZIKER INC
208 3rd Avenue South
Seattle
Washington 98104
USA
Tel: + 1 (206) 467 1144

TODHUNTER EARLE
Chelsea Reach
79-89 Lots Road
London SW10 0RN
England
Tel: + 44 (0) 20 7349 9999
todhunterearle.com

TRISTAN AUER
5a cour de la Métaine
75020 Paris
France
Tel: + 33 (0) 1 43 49 57 20

VICENTE WOLF ASSOCIATES
333 West 39th Street
New York NY 10019
USA
Tel: + 1 (212) 465 0590
vicentewolfassociates.com

VINCENT VAN DUYSEN
Lombardenvest 34
2000 Antwerp
Belgium
Tel: + 32 (0) 3 205 9190
vanduysen.be

VIRGINIE GRAVIERE &
OLIVIER MARTIN
139 rue Belleville
33000 Bordeaux
France
Tel: + 33 (0) 5 5698 2381
Martin.graviere@wanadoo.fr

WELLS MACKERETH
ARCHITECTS
5e Shepherd Street
Mayfair
London W1J 7HP
England
Tel: +44 (0) 20 7495 7044
wellsmackereth.com

Picture Acknowledgements

PHOTOGRAPHERS' CREDITS

Giorgio Baroni
101

Ken Hayden
56, 71, 89 below left, 100 right, 105 above right, 119

David Ross
54

Simon Upton
Back jacket top right and below, page 1, 3, 5, 7, 11 above right, 11 below right, 14-15, 20-21, 26 right, 28-29, 30, 32 left, 33, 36, 37, 41 above left & right, 41 centre left & right, 43, 45, 47 left, 51-53, 55, 58-59, 61, 64, 66, 72, 74, 76-77, 78, 80 left, 81, 82-87, 89 above left & right, 92, 93, 95, 97, 98, 99 right, 102, 103, 106, 112, 113 right 114 above, 115-117, 120, 122-123, 125-128, 130-132, 135, 144

Frederic Vasseur
17 below right, 18, 27, 41 below right, 44 left, 60 below, 91 below left, 94 right, 111, 133

Luke White
Front jacket, back jacket above left, 32 right, 50, 73, 100 left, 105 above left & below right, 129

Andrew Wood:
Back jacket top centre, endpapers; 2, 4, 8-9, 11 above left, centre & below left, 12-13, 16, 17 above left & right, 17 below left, 19, 22-23, 24, 25, 26 left, 31, 34-35, 38-39, 41 below right, 43, 44 right, 46, 47 right, 48-49, 57, 60 above, 62-63, 65, 67-69, 70, 75, 79, 80 right, 89 centre left & right and below right, 92, 94 left, 96, 99 left, 105 below left, 107, 108, 109, 110, 113 left, 114 below, 118, 121, 134

LOCATION CREDITS

Front Jacket creations and style by Catherine Memmi, Paris, own home in Normandy

Back jacket top left: a house in Bridgehampton, designed by Vicente Wolf; top centre: Anna Bonde's house in Provence; top right: Tigmi, Morocco, designed by Max Lawrence; below left: Peter and Marijke de Wit of Domaine d'Heerstaayen in the Netherlands; below centre: a mountain retreat in Colorado, designed by Ron Mason; below right: Alastair Gordon & Barbara de Vries' home in New Jersey.

Front endpapers: a house in North Province, South Africa, designed by Collett-Zarzycki Architects & Designers. Back endpapers: a house in Johannesburg, designed by Johann Slee.

1 a home featuring Jane Churchill fabrics; 2 a house in Bordeaux, designed by Virginie Gravière & Olivier Martin; 4 Nigel Greenwood's apartment in London; 5 Ali Sharland's house in Gloucestershire; 7 Alastair Gordon & Barbara de Vries' home in New Jersey; 8-9 a house in the Hamptons designed by Solis Betancourt; 11 above left Johann Slee's home in Johannesburg, 11 above right Axel Vervoordt's house in Belgium; 11 centre left Richard & Lucille Lewin's house In Plettenberg Bay South Africa, designed by Seth Stein; 11 centre right a house in Marrakech, designed by Karl Fournier and Olivier Marty, Studio KO; 11 below left Anthony Hudson's barn in Norfolk; 11 below right a house in Connecticut designed by Jeffrey Bilhuber; 12-13 a house in Marrakech, designed by Karl Fournier and Olivier Marty, Studio KO; 14 Mr and Mrs Stokke's cabin in the Norwegian mountains, interior design by Helene Forbes-Hennie; 16 above Van Breestraat residence, Amsterdam, designed by Marc Prosman Architecten Bv; 16 below Weaving/Thomasson residence, London; 17 above left a house in Victoria, Australia, designed by Black Kosloff Knott; 17 above right Steven Ehrlich, FAIA's house in Venice, California; 17 below left a house in Brooklyn, New York designed by Ogawa Depardon Architects; 17 below right William Cumming's house on Long Island, designed by William Cummings at Heiberg Cummings Design; 18 a house in Suffolk designed by James Gorst; 19 Johann Slee's house in Johannesburg; 20 Peter and Marijke de Wit of Domaine d'Heerstaayen in the Netherlands; 21 a mountain retreat in Colorado, designed by Ron Mason; 22 Anthony Hudson's barn in Norfolk; 23 Pam Skaist-Levy of Juicy Couture's house designed by Leonardo Chalupowicz; 24 Johann Slee's home in Johannesburg; 25 Keith & Cathy Abell's New York house designed by 1100 Architect; 26 left Patrick Clifford's house in Auckland designed by Architectus; 27 Ben Cherner & Emma O'Neill's apartment in New York, designed by Emma O'Neill; 28 Mrs Fasting's cabin in the Norwegian mountains, interior design by Heiberg Cummings Design; 29 James Gager & Richard Ferretti's Pennsylvanian house; 30 a house featuring Jane Churchill fabrics; 31 Anthony Hudson's barn in Norfolk; 32 left Ali Sharland's house in Gloucestershire; 32 right a house in Bridgehampton, designed by Vicente Wolf; 33 left Josephine Ryan's house in London; 33 right Alastair Gordon & Barbara de Vries' home in New Jersey; 34 a house in the Hamptons designed by Solis Betancourt; 34-35 a house in Bordeaux, designed by Virginie Gravière & Olivier Martin; 36 Axel Vervoordt's house in Belgium; 37 left Dominique Kieffer's house in Normandy; 37 right Alastair Gordon & Barbara de Vries' home in New Jersey; 38-39 Richard & Lucille Lewin's house in London, designed by Seth Stein; 41 above left Ivy Ross & Brian Gill's home in Galisteo; 41 above right a home featuring Jane Churchill fabrics; 41 centre left Wingate Jackson, Jr and Paul Trantanella's house in upstate New York; 41 centre right Axel Vervoordt's house in Belgium; 41 below left an apartment in Paris, designed by Studio K O; 41 below right Lena Proudlock's house in Gloucestershire; 42 a house in Ibiza, designed by Ramón Esteve Architects; 43 a mountain retreat in Colorado, designed by Ron Mason; 44 left James Falla & Lynn Graham's house in Guernsey, designed by James Falla at MOOArc; 44 right a house in New South Wales designed by Clinton Murray; 45 designed by Stickland Coombe Architecture; 46 Richard & Lucille Lewin's House In Plettenberg Bay South Africa, designed by Seth Stein; 47 left a mountain retreat in Colorado, designed by Ron Mason; 47 right an apartment in

Brussels designed by Vincent van Duysen; 48-49 Sally Mackereth & Julian Vogel's house in London, designed by Wells Mackereth; 50 created and styled by Catherine Memmi, Paris, own home in Normandy; 51 Alex van de Walle's apartment in Brussels; 52 above Axel Vervoordt's house in Belgium; 52 below Peter and Marijke de Wit of Domaine d'Heerstaayen in the Netherlands; 53 James Gager & Richard Ferretti's Pennsylvanian house; 54 a house in South Africa, designed by Stephen Falcke; 57 above left & below right a house in the Hamptons designed by Solis Betancourt; 57 above right & below left Anna Bonde's house in Provence; 58-59 Axel Vervoordt's house in Belgium; 60 above Mark Rios's home in Los Angeles; 60 below Ben Cherner & Emma O'Neill's apartment in New York, designed by Emma O'Neill; 61 Hanne Kjaerholm's house in Copenhagen; 62-63 Robert Kaiser residence, Florida, designed by Gene Leedy architect; 64 right James Gager & Richard Ferretti's Pennsylvanian house; 65 left Weaving/Thomasson residence, London; 65 right Mark Rios's home in Los Angeles; 67 Jocelyn & Simon Warner's house in London; 68 Patrick Clifford's house in Auckland designed by Architectus; 69 left an apartment in Paris designed by Frédéric Méchiche; 69 right Tristan Auer's apartment in Paris; 70 left John and Marilyn Roscoe's house in California, designed by Helena Arahuete Architect of Lautner Associates; 70 right a house in Delhi, designed by Abraham & Thakore; 71 interior designer Daniel Romualdez, New York; 73 a riverside apartment in London, designed by Luigi Esposito; 74 left Alex van de Walle's apartment in Brussels; 74 right a house featuring Jane Churchill fabrics; 75 Muriel Brandolini's home in the Hamptons, New York; 76 Emma Hawkins' house in Edinburgh; 77 left Jerry & Maxine Swartz's house in Germantown, New York, designed by Frank Faulkner; 77 right Laurent Dombrowicz & Franck Delmarcelle's house in Northern France; 79 Graham Head (of ABC Carpet & Home) and Barbara Rathborne's house in Long Island; 80 left a home featuring Jane Churchill fabrics; 80 right Graham Head (of ABC Carpet & Home) and Barbara

Rathborne's house in Long Island; 81 a home featuring Jane Churchill fabrics; 82-83 Lena Proudlock of Denim In Style's house in Gloucestershire; 84 Lena Proudlock's house in Gloucestershire; 85 left a home featuring Jane Churchill fabrics; 85 right Lena Proudlock's house in Gloucestershire; 86-87 Peter and Marijke de Wit of Domaine d'Heerstaayen in the Netherlands; 89 above left a home featuring Jane Churchill fabrics; 89 above right James Gager & Richard Ferretti's Pennsylvanian house; 89 centre left Mark Badgley and James Mischka's New York apartment; 89 centre right Nigel Greenwood's apartment in London; 89 below left designed by Jean-Dominique Bonhotal; 89 below right Nigel Greenwood's apartment in London; 90 a house in Connecticut designed by Jeffrey Bilhuber; 91 above left Johann Slee's home in Johannesburg; 91 above right a house near Grasse, France, designed by Collett-Zarzycki Architects & Designers; 91 below left James Falla & Lynn Graham's house in Guernsey, designed by James Falla at MOOArc; 91 below right Anthony Hudson's barn in Norfolk; 92 A house in the Hamptons designed by Solis Betancourt; 93 home of Peri Wolfman and Charles Gold in Bridgehampton; 94 left Paolo Badesco's villa in Italy; 94 right Ben Cherner & Emma O'Neill's apartment in New York, designed by Emma O'Neill; 95 Ivy Ross & Brian Gill's home in Galisteo; 96 Eric Gizard's apartment in Paris; 97 a mountain retreat in Colorado, designed by Ron Mason; 98 left Mr & Mrs Stokke's cabin in the Norwegian mountains, interior design by Helene Forbes-Hennie; 98 right Ben Langlands & Nikki Bell's house in London; 99 left A house in New York designed by Shelton, Mindel & Associates; 99 right architect Gilles Pellerin's house in Cannes; 100 left a house in Bridgehampton, designed by Vicente Wolf; 101 designer Alberto Pinto; 102 a home featuring Jane Churchill fabrics; 103 left Althea Wilson's house in London; 103 right Michael Leva's house in Connecticut; 105 above left a riverside apartment in London, designed by Luigi Esposito; 105 above right designed by Jonathan Reed; 105 below left Ralph & Ann Pucci's New York home, furnished in collaboration with Vicente Wolf; 105

below right Bernie de le Cuona's London showroom; 106 a home featuring Jane Churchill fabrics; 107 Anna Bonde's house in Provence; 108 a house in Delhi, designed by Abraham & Thakore; 109 a house in North Province, South Africa, designed by Collett-Zarzycki Architects & Designers; 110 left A house in Delhi, designed by Abraham & Thakore; 110 right a house in North Province, South Africa, designed by Collett-Zarzycki Architects & Designers; 111 Nina Gustafsson's Swedish home; 112 a home featuring Jane Churchill fabrics; 113 left a house in the Hamptons designed by Solis Betancourt; 114 above Michael Leva's house in Connecticut; 114 below Jasper Conran's home in London; 115 Axel Vervoordt's house in Belgium; 116 left Axel Vervoordt's house in Belgium; 116 right Ali Sharland's house in Gloucestershire; 117 a house in Oxfordshire designed by Todhunter Earle; 118 Johann Slee's home in Johannesburg; 119 designed by Terry Hunziker; 120 right Axel Vervoordt's house in Belgium; 121 left Pam Skaist-Levy of Juicy Couture's house designed by Leonardo Chalupowicz; 121 right a house in Balnarring in coastal Victoria, designed by John Wardle Architects; 125 above left Rupert & Caroline Spira's house in Shropshire; 125 above right a home featuring Jane Churchill fabrics; 125 centre left designed by Pierre d'Avoine Architects; 125 below left Hubert Zandberg's apartment in London; 126 Rupert & Caroline Spira's house in Shropshire; 127 above left Charles Worthington's house in Kent; 127 above right Alex van de Walle's apartment in Brussels; 127 below left a house in Provence designed by Jean-Louis Raynaud & Kenyon Kramer; 127 below right Peter Adler's house in London; 128 a house in Connecticut designed by Jeffrey Bilhuber; 129 a house in Bridgehampton, designed by Vicente Wolf; 131 Peter Adler's house in London; 132 Alex van de Walle's apartment in Brussels; 133 Nina Gustafsson's Swedish home; 134 a house in the Hamptons designed by Solis Betancourt; 135 Julie Prisca's house in Normandy; 144 Peter and Marijke de Wit of Domaine d'Heerstaayen in the Netherlands.

Acknowledgements

Thank you, Jacqui, for asking me to write a book on the natural home.
It is the hot topic of our times, one that we should all embrace and
weave into our everyday lives. Many thanks also to Jo at Jacqui Small,
for her very efficient support, and to Hilary, Ash and Nadine, whose
combined creative and pin-sharp skills have been the making of this
book. And finally, thanks to my family, Anthony, Cicely and Felix –
brand new converts to a greener way of life!